Letters, notes, long-distance phone calls, and
an excited grandmother be-ribboned as a
Christmas gift at the Miami airport—all tell
a fabulous "now" kind of love story.

The second time Frances Gardner Hunter met
her husband-to-be was only a few hours before their minute-after-midnight wedding on
New Year's Day. This book is the intimate
love-letter account of their amazing phone
and mail courtship. Every detail of their
Divinely-arranged love and marriage is to
Frances and Charles the result of their one
desire—to do God's will. Theirs is a re-
freshingly honest story of overflowing life
and love in Jesus Christ.

My Love Affair With Charles

BY FRANCES GARDNER HUNTER

A Division of G/L Publications
Glendale, California, U.S.A.

Other books by Frances Hunter—

God Is Fabulous
Hot Line to Heaven
Go, Man, Go

Scripture quoted from the *Authorized Version;*
New Testament in Modern English (Phillips
translation), copyrighted by J. B. Phillips,
1958 and used by permission of the Macmillan
Company; *Revised Standard Version of the Bible,*
copyrighted 1946 and 1952, Division of Christian
Education, N.C.C.C., U.S.A.

Published by
Regal Books Division, G/L Publications
Glendale, California 91209, U.S.A.

Library of Congress Catalog Card No. 72-150717
Hardcover edition: ISBN 0-8307-0099-4
Paperback edition: ISBN 0-8307-0098-6

TO MY BELOVED CHARLES,

This book is dedicated with all of
the love that God has poured into me for you
. . . but then how could I help but love
you when God engineered it all!

Foreword

(The manuscript for *My Love Affair with Charles* was sent by the author to Pat Boone for review. Since he was out of town when the manuscript arrived, Shirley Boone decided to read it and then share her reactions to the manuscript with husband Pat.)

November 15, 1970

Dearest Pat:

I have just read Frances' manuscript, *My Love Affair with Charles* and I just have to share it with you! Here are two people who lost their first mates, and because they put Jesus first in their lives He supplied all their needs. He gave them a new and fresh love that just comes alive on the pages. It's really been *fun* to read!

Frances tells this story in such a beautiful way. We know this love comes from Jesus because He's the one who renewed *our* love, and this is one of the reasons I'd like people to share with Frances' and Charles' experiences—it might help heal a lot of marriages that have not found that putting God first is a healing balm for a shaky marriage.

Some of the things I like are their sense of humor, dedication and childlike love and faith—a real spiritual excitement. They make it high adventure to have God in their relationship. How wonderful it is to know that there is another couple in the Lord who are experiencing the same kind of love and sweetness that we have . . . that the Lord has brought them together in this way. The only common denominator between Frances and Charles and Shirley and Pat is Jesus Christ—but what a glorious bond!

God's love is what this world needs! Praise God for those who are willing to share what He's done for them. Let me know what you think.

I love you . . .
Shirley

*   *   *

November 17, 1970

Hi Honey!

You're right! Frances' and Charles' manuscript is rich! It's not so much a book as it is an intimate glimpse into the anatomy of a Divinely nurtured love affair.

As you can imagine, I sat here in the hotel room laughing and crying by turns, eagerly "eavesdropping" while the two of them fell in love, fought it, denied it, rationalized it, realized it—and finally accepted and thanked God for His goodness in giving them each other!

I don't know what there is about reading other people's letters; even when a lot of people are mentioned that have no faces for you, there's a built-in intrigue. Your mind tends to fill in the gaps, in probably a more interesting fashion than the actual facts. I used to enjoy "Gunsmoke" on the radio more than I do now on TV; I think it's because my mind created more exciting detail than the Hollywood set designer. Anyway, for some reason, I got more of a bona fide kick out of reading the Hunters' letters, even with the "loose end" mentions of people and events, than most carefully constructed novels I've read.

Maybe it's because God constructed the plot!

He knew that these two were putting Him first in all things, and in turn, what would complete and fulfill them. I watched Him accept their unselfish love as individuals and then weld them into one flesh. In a much smaller, but more personal 20th century way, I found myself making a comparison between these letters and the book of Acts—in both cases, the fascination comes as you realize that you're watching the Holy Spirit at work, in His perfect, unerring way!

If only every married couple in the world would discover the fantastic symphony God is anxious to compose with their lives and their yielded spirits! If only they could glimpse, as you and I have, the impossibility of achieving complete "oneness" without separate and mutual surrender to God's precious Spirit. Surely the Hunters' book will provide such an exciting glimpse for many frustrated twosomes.

Thank God for them, for hteir book, for His omniscience—and for you! I love you even more after reading this book!

Be home soon,
Pat

Author's Introduction

This is a love story. Not really *a* love story, but *my* love story. But then as I think of it, it really isn't *my* love story, but a story of God's love. It happened this very year in the lives of two very ordinary people who were twelve hundred miles apart, yet drawn to God by the same powerful force in total dedication, and then drawn to each other by God.

I dare you to read this love story and ever be the same.

These are some of the people you will meet in Charles' and my letters—

FRANCES (That's me): Many of you may have read the story of how I became a Christian at the age of 49 *(God Is Fabulous)*—and from the moment I became a Christian I have had no desire for anything except the things of God. The gentle touch of Jesus upon my life completely transformed my every action, thought and attitude within a short period of time. Since then I have traveled across the United States sharing my wild enthusiasm for the man Jesus Christ.

CHARLES (My husband): His story is quite different from mine. He had sat in a church as an excellent "church member," treasurer and holder of every office possible, but in his own words he was a "dried-up spiritual prune." And then about two and a half years ago, he knelt at an altar about 6:30 in the morning, and without music, a sermon or any type of emotional appeal, he felt a tremendous drawing to God, and simply asked God, "Take all of my life and make me spiritually what you want me to be." Nothing happened for four months, and then all of a sudden changes began occurring. There came a fantastic desire to read the Word of God, a greater desire to pray more than ever before in his life and a desire for nothing except more, more, more of God. Charles is a CPA and partner in a firm in Houston, Texas.

JEANNE: Charles' deceased wife, and half of a beautiful marriage that ended in a beautiful death because of Christ becoming a reality in their lives. Many of the exciting experiences in Charles' tremendous growing period occurred as he and Jeanne together surrendered their total lives to God.

TOM: My 25-year-old son who has not yet discovered that the answer to life lies in the man Christ Jesus.

JAN: My daughter-in-law.

BRANT: My grandson.

MOLLY, JUNE and SUE: Friends of Charles whom God used in the fleece I put out.

JOAN: My 16- (now 17-) year-old daughter who is now OUR daughter, having been adopted by Charles.

GRANDMA: My mother-in-law who accepted Christ as her personal Saviour at the age of 86.

JESUS CHRIST: The most exciting man I ever met and with whom I'm going to have a mad wild love affair the rest of my life. He is the one who gave me Charles.

*I*T ALL BEGAN with a telephone call! And little did any of us realize what this phone call would lead to and how God himself must have dialed the number that night.

I had been out on the visitation program of our church, and returned to my office late one night to catch up on some work, and one of my employees said to me, "You've got a long distance call to return—a Mr. Charles Hunter in Houston, Texas." At that particular time I had been receiving an unusual number of phone calls (often in the middle of the night) from people with all kinds of interesting little quirks about Christianity. (Just write a few books and speak all over the country, and the same thing

1

will happen to you.) Anyway I dismissed the call with a flat statement of "It's probably not important!" But the next night the call was repeated . . . again I was out . . . and again the lady in my office said, "That Mr. Hunter called again—he says it's urgent!" Again I dismissed it with "If it's really urgent he'll call again." Then on the third night I returned the call.

Mr. Hunter said he had read where I was going to be in the Houston area and that he had been inspired by my book "God Is Fabulous," and he asked me to speak to a group of young people. I advised him that since I was coming to Houston to be the Religious Emphasis Week speaker at a Christian college the schedule was being made out by the president of the college, so it would be necessary to contact him for any speaking date.

Then Mr. Hunter told me that his wife had died during the last year, and probably a few other statements which I didn't listen to too well, and then he said, "I have a large house in Houston, and I'd like to have you make it your headquarters while you're in Houston." I didn't know Mr. Hunter, or anything about him, or the kind of a person he was, so I really raised my eyebrows at that remark and very coldly said, "No, thank you! My housing arrangements have been made by the college!" And with that I hung up the telephone very indignantly, not even hearing Mr. Hunter's reassurance of a Christian housekeeper. I then turned to the lady in my office and said, "That dirty old man, do you know what he wanted? He wanted me to stay at his house while I'm in Houston." Then I really felt very righteous and said, "Who does he think *HE* is, and what does he think *I* am?" And with that I dismissed Charles Hunter from my mind. (So I thought.)

My tour to Houston started in Oklahoma and I had a wild exciting time there seeing many victories for the Lord, and was really wound up when I got to Houston. The first thing I did was to go to the office of the college president (Max Gaulke) to pick up my schedule. And to show you the Lord was working even then—when the president handed me the schedule, which was two pages long, I immediately flipped over to the second page to see if Mr. Hunter's name was there. AND IT WAS! I narrowed my eyes and thought, "Wait until I meet him, I'll freeze him out!" But nevertheless something had made me look to see if his name was there.

On Friday night after an exciting week in Houston, I walked into the church where I was to speak that night, and the minister said, "I have someone very special I'd like you to meet!" I thought, "Here we go again!" It seems that every pastor always had "someone very special" they wanted me to meet (they weren't content to have me unmarried). And then he said, "I want you to meet Charles Hunter."

I immediately switched on my icicle-making machine and then turned to shake hands with this Mr. Hunter. As I shook his hand the most amazing thing happened! NEVER IN MY LIFE HAS THE SPIRIT OF GOD IN MY BODY BLENDED WITH THE SPIRIT OF GOD IN ANOTHER PERSON LIKE IT DID WITH CHARLES HUNT-ER! I stood there completely enveloped in the power

*of God's Holy Spirit and for two solid minutes I
didn't say a word. Charles didn't say a word. . . . The
pastor didn't say a word. . . . The three of us were
completely under the spell of God's Holy Spirit. I
didn't even realize what was happening. All of a
sudden I remember looking at my hand which was
holding Charles' and I thought, "What's that in his
hand?" And then I remember thinking, "It looks like
my hand!" I remember taking my hand away without
saying a word and looking at it and wondering what
to do with it, so I just quickly put my hand behind
me. To the best of my knowledge there were no other
words spoken because it was time to start the church
service.*

*I didn't talk to Charles that night because I left
after the service to go to a prayer meeting in one of
the college dorms, but the next morning I spoke at a
breakfast and guess who was the first one I saw
there? You're right . . . Charles. I didn't say more
than one or two sentences to him (just enough to tell
him what time he could pick me up the next day to
speak to the young people in his church) because I
left immediately after the breakfast to speak at a
mission in Houston.*

*Sunday he was right on time and we left to drive to
the church where I was to speak, and it took me only
a few minutes to discover that Charles was not a
"dirty old man" at all, but the most exciting Christian I had ever met. He shared with me how he had
sat in a church for thirty years (I'm quoting him, and
not just talking behind his back) as a spiritual
"dried-up prune," and then how in the last year and
a half Christ had become a reality in his life—and*

Christ had become a living, moving force in his life and how he had really come ALIVE in Christ! It was so exciting just listening to someone tell of the miracles that Christ was doing in his life daily that I nearly burst.

After speaking at the one church, Charles brought me back to another church where we had a fabulous three-hour service. When the service was over, Charles somehow or other got through the crowd that surrounded me and all of a sudden I remembered I had promised Bill Menefee, Lay Leader for Campus Crusade for Christ, that I would visit him during the week, and here it was, my last night in Houston, and I hadn't been able to see him.

I looked at Charles and asked, "Do you know where . . . is?"

And he said, "No, but I'll be glad to help you find it!"

I then asked, "Are you available?" The words really floored me because I had asked an utter stranger (except we weren't really strangers because he was my brother in Christ) if he was available that night. But Charles said, "Yes, I'm available." So I said, "Let's go!"

We started out to find the address I had given Charles, but when we found it, the house was all dark, and obviously everyone was in bed. I just knew I couldn't go back to Miami without having met Bill Menefee, so I told Charles to stay in the car and I got out real fast and knocked on the door. Then all of a sudden I realized the Menefees might not appreciate my waking them up, so I began to pray audibly (I'm not a secret service Christian). I said, "Lord, let his

Christianity be in real good shape tonight so he won't be mad at me." And about the time I finished praying I noticed that Charles had gotten out of the car and was standing beside me with the most puzzled look on his face. He said, "I don't believe it . . . I don't believe it . . . I just don't believe that Christians do things like this." And then listen to what he said, "I feel like I'm living a chapter in your next book." Little did he realize what he was saying! (He got the WHOLE book, didn't he?)

The door opened and I said, "Praise the Lord, I'm Frances Gardner." And God had answered my prayer because Bill Menefee's Christianity was in its usual good shape and he said, "Praise the Lord, come on in."

Bill got his wife Suzanne out of bed and the four of us sat there for about three hours just sharing the miracles that Christ had done in our lives, and what a glorious time we had. About two in the morning Charles took me back to the apartment where I was staying and we sat in the car and prayed. During the prayer, Charles prayed: "Lord, since everything I have is yours, let her know that if she ever needs anything or runs into a problem while on tour, everything I have is also hers because of her dedication to you." When the prayer concluded, Charles stuck a business card in my pocketbook so I would know how to get in touch with him, and before we finally finished talking about the miracles of God he somehow or other had managed to put twenty-seven business cards in my pocketbook. (He wanted to make sure I knew how to get in touch with him if I needed him.)

The next morning the president of the college picked me up to take me to the airport and on the way we talked of the exciting things that had happened at the college during the past week. As he put me on the plane he made a most unusual statement. You'd have to know the president of the college to appreciate what he said because he's very austere and proper and never under any circumstances would he say anything the least bit out of the way. But he looked right at me and said, "Frances, I think you ought to marry some rich man so you can travel all around without worrying about money." This shocked me, but the words the Lord put in my mouth shocked me even more, because I said, "I believe you and Charles Hunter have the same idea."

I COULDN'T BELIEVE I'D SAID IT! I didn't even know Charles Hunter and yet here I was making a grand statement like this. But having said it, I commented no more. And neither did the college president. (Charles says the only thing that was wrong was that the president said a RICH man.)

I remember as the huge jet took off and circled back over Houston I looked out the window and secretly wondered which office building Charles Hunter's office was in and then my heart really flip-flopped or something because I looked up and cried out, "Lord, you didn't throw me a curve, did you?" At that time I felt there was no time in my life for love, romance or marriage because of the call God had put on my life, but I guess I knew even then that I had left a part of my heart in Houston.

I thought no more about Charles Hunter until I got home, and the first thing I did was to call my

7

pastor because I always kept him informed of all the miracles en route and on trips, but this time I said something different. I said, "Rev. Slagle, I met a man who didn't turn me off . . . now don't worry . . . he didn't turn me on, but he didn't turn me off." And my beloved pastor said even then he wondered what had happened, because in all the years he had known me he had never heard me say anything like that before.

Immediately after that I went to the office and wrote the following letter to Charles.

* * *

Miami, Florida, October 9, 1969

Dear Charles:

Just a real quickie note as I try to fight my way out of the mess my desk was in when I got back, to let you know how grateful I am to have had the opportunity of meeting you and sharing in your church and just sharing some Christian excitement with you.

I absolutely can't unwind from my trip because it was so exciting from beginning to end. When I left Houston I went on to the Christian Women's Club in Orlando and there I saw God's Holy Spirit move in a great and mighty way. Sixty-eight decision tags were turned in. P.T.L.

And then Cinderella had to come back home and be a working girl again. I'm getting ready to go to West Virginia and Pennsylvania next week. I'll be leaving early Friday morning and will be gone another ten days. I was a little disturbed when I realized I had booked two tours so close together, but I realize now this is part of God's plan to release me from this office. The effect on my son seems to be real great—but then how could it be otherwise when it's God's idea.

I ordered the 2,000 "Four Spiritual Law" booklets which are being sent to Gulf Coast, and I had them billed to you. I told Max when he took me to the plane that you were donating them. I think it's just marvelous, and so does he! I'm just praying that those kids stay on fire and I pray for them nightly. Include a little prayer for them, will you?

I sent you an album today so you can be looking for that, and if you have time, you might also include me in your prayers. I hope you realize the gratitude in my heart for your most generous gift—this really helped me know and believe even more than ever before that my God will supply my every need.

In His exciting service,

Frances

* * *

AUTHOR'S NOTE: This letter might have never made history except for one fact—I'm NOT a letter writer! As often as I had been gone on trips from home, I had never written a letter to my family. I called them often during a trip, but NEVER did I write letters because I just don't happen to like writing letters.

And as if that were not enough—to write a letter when you're not a letter writer—the next morning I sat right down and wrote a second letter.

9

Miami, Florida
October 11, 1969

<small>PRAISE THE LORD   PRAISE THE LORD   PRAISE THE LORD</small>

Dear Charles:

Just a real quickie note tonight to let you know that I'm really praying for you and all the young people who prayed to receive Christ last Sunday afternoon. It doesn't seem possible it was just a short week ago that I was in Houston.

I have such a great burden for these young people because these decisions have got to be fed or they'll just wither and die, so I'm praying that God will give you the wisdom to know what to do. Have you ever used "Ten Steps to Christian Maturity" by Campus Crusade for Christ? It's excellent!

Even though I'm gone so much of the time, I'm still praying for 100 in my Sunday School class before the end of the year. And talking about the end of the year, last New Year's Eve we had a P.T.L. (Party for the Lord) which was just fabulous (where have I heard that word before?) and we're having another one this New Year's Eve. If you're going to be free that evening, you might want to spend it with the Lord in Miami. I'll guarantee you the most spiritual night of your life. We're going to have people from various places in the United States coming, and we're excited about it.

Wish I had time to write about the exciting miracles I see every day—but will just have to write another book *instead*. In the meantime, please let me know how the young people are doing and please also know that I'm really praying for you.

Because He loves, I love,
Frances

P.S. Here's a little book that Charles Weber wrote a long time ago that I like and give to new converts. It has some great spiritual truths in it. You might try assigning them a verse a week to memorize.

*   *   *

AUTHOR'S NOTE: After I mailed this letter I couldn't believe I had written two letters to a man I really didn't know, except I felt I had known him my whole life because of our shared relationship to Christ. Even though I was amazed that I had written and asked him to come to Miami for a New Year's Party, I don't think I ever believed he really would come. Nevertheless I was completely shocked that I had asked an utter stranger to spend the money necessary to come from Houston to Miami for a matter of a few hours. . . . Think of the complete improbability of the situation. You just don't ask people to come 1,200 miles for a 3-, 4- or 5-hour party, do you? Maybe you wouldn't, but God does.

I knew that Charles wouldn't accept the invitation to come to the party since there was so much distance involved, and then decided I didn't have time to write any more letters to him anyway, but very shortly came an answer (and I had to be polite and answer, didn't I?) . . . Now watch the tempo and the number of letters increase.

Houston, Texas 77024—October 16, 1969

Dear Frances,

Boy, does God know how to run His business! Tonite no action was ahead so I had a nite to read. My greatest joy seems to come after two or three hours in an evening reading the Bible. But, hayfever settled in my eyes and I could do very little reading, so He (and you were his helper) sent me a record and you don't need eyes to see Christ. Thanks for sending it. I heard side 1 and will listen to side 2 when He's ready—tonite or another nite—but this letter comes next. The record's great!

I hope you find a lot of people (or at least a few) in your travels who really find excitement every day in the little and big things God does without any effort you make except to "hang loose." It gets greater every week. Without trying to write a book, I'll just tell one thing that happened Sunday which is not unlike so many of God's ways.

It started in Sunday School class—our teacher announced that if Tom Smith, who was responsible for appropriately utilizing a Bible-teaching film, could find a moderator for Sunday nite, they would start a 13-week showing of the film with a discussion following. Now, that isn't exciting, is it? But wait. Next, I went to the choir room before the morning service and a lady came to me to invite me to her home for Sunday dinner and I accepted. That isn't particularly exciting (it's nice) but I can generally expect something to break loose on Sunday especially, so I felt things were picking up. Next, when church started I stopped long enough to realize I had a sore throat and stopped-up head and this family had four children who didn't need my sore throat, so, I said, "Lord, if you really want me to go, have my throat well by the end of the service." You know it, not a sign of soreness at 12:00 o'clock, so off to their home for dinner. We had a lovely dinner, a good visit (my first time to know them more than casually) and as I shared some excerpts from Jeanne's and my experience, the man and his wife both grew excited because they felt the excitement God has given me (and you know what that really means) and expressed how they wished they could feel this.

Before I left about 4:00 P.M., God put all his pieces together to make a puzzle into an orderly picture. The man was Tom Smith who needed a moderator for the Bible discussion on Sunday night and God had Mrs. Smith invite me to dinner, without any of us knowing what was taking place, but he said he felt so strongly that I should be one of the moderators! Now I wouldn't dare say no. Oh, yes, when I left their home, my sore throat came back, but it really didn't matter. God really is fabulous! PTL.

By the way, we are rehearsing the "Hallelujah Chorus" and when 65 voices sing "Praise the Lord," it's great and means even more to me because of your PTL pep rally!

It was great to get personally acquainted with you. Really of all the people I've been around for the past five months you are the only Christian who has demonstrated the excitement I have felt. Sad isn't it that so few have this thrill. I guess there are a lot more but God scattered them around. It is a great gift and I'm humbled to have received so abundantly from him. How could I do less than turn loose of everything and let him run my life.

I keep hearing from many sources the impact and impression God made on my church through you. Many people have expressed their appreciation. I know Christ entered many hearts and in God's time we will know which ones. Sunday morning the mother of a 17-year-old girl who heard you, talked to me about how much this meant to her daughter. She didn't say what her daughter had experienced a year ago but I felt she had seen a miracle in her life and it seemed she was confused as to what to believe, but her mother said your talk (it was a lot more than a talk) seemed to straighten it all out in her mind. PTL! I told her I would love to meet and talk with her daughter.

I appreciate your taking time to write not just one, but two letters. I like the way you quit working 20 hours a day on tour and became a "working gal" again in Miami!

About your books: Miss Edes has them. I bought 50 of them to give away.

You asked if I had used the "Ten Steps. . . ." No, but I will get info from Campus Crusade. I have also for about three months had a burden and a great, deep love for these young people and know God will do a great job in their lives. Please pray often for His direction—I know He will lead.

As I see action I will keep you advised and will (and have been) keep praying for daily miracles in your life—and "you ain't seen nothing yet!"

This letter is too long, so I promise to stop soon. Please know that, as I told you, I own no part of my finances and if in your fully dedicated work you have any need anywhere, if I have it and you need it, God will provide. This is not limited to the purchase of "Four Spiritual Laws" wherever you need them, but to any need. You know I'm not financially rich, but what I have is the Lord's.

With greatest excitement I have ever known, I say, Goodnite and my prayers are with you.

Love,
Charles

PTL   TURN LOOSE

Thanks for the invitation to your New Year's Eve PTL. You just never know what God's next move may be, so if you see a foreigner there, it could be me! I know it will be fabulous!

*   *   *

Houston, Texas 77024
10-30-69

Dear Frances:

WOW!! Just must write a short note about at least tonite's thrill! You remember the little Christian Women's Mission—Mrs. Toliver and the *one* you were sent to. Jesus Christ visited them again tonite and used my voice for a great evening. One said she gave her heart to Jesus. It touched several of them and one lady asked for prayer for her son (brain damage). The miracle of this is not whether God heals her son but this is the first time she has asked any of them to pray for any of her needs, and so God is beginning a healing of her soul and replacing some resentment with love. How have you stood 3½ years of this fabulous life. I have only had 5 months and if each month keeps getting more exciting than the one before I may just explode—if I do, God can put me back together again.

So many thrilling things have happened that I'm going to have to install a "mouth closer" or I'll talk everyone to death, or rather to life. The Holy Spirit really does a great job when you turn loose and let Him use your "facilities."

I will be in Lake Charles 12/17/69 and will love to speak to 28 new and used (improved) Christians you left. This should be fun because life really is fun with Christ.

The 2,000 "Four Spiritual Law" booklets must have arrived at GBC—I received notice and paid for them today, so I'll expect the 400 you said would find Christ.

Lots of exciting love in Christ,
Charles

* * *

AUTHOR'S NOTE: I left on tour for two weeks, therefore no letters were written during this time.

However, a peculiar thing had happened to me. I had developed the most uncontrollable urge to share everything with this man I didn't even know except through Christ, and when I returned from one of the most exciting tours of my career, I was utterly compelled to place a long-distance call to Charles. No one answered the telephone, so I waited for approximately an hour and then prayed, "Lord, if you want

16

me to share with Charles Hunter the miracles of this trip, let him be home RIGHT NOW. If not, then see that he's still out, because I only want what you want."

This time when the phone rang, Charles had just come in the door.

* * *

November 2, 1969, 6:30 AM

Dear Frances,

God is really terrific!

He really gives a lot of variety and maybe that's part of the reason life is so exciting. What a way to end a perfect day—getting a call from the second most exciting person I know at midnight your time. I don't have to tell you who No. 1 excitement is!

Just read a very descriptive paragraph in Ephesians 1:15-21: "That God, the God of our Lord Jesus Christ and the all-glorious Father, will give you spiritual wisdom and the insight to know more of him; that you may receive that inner illumination of the spirit which will make you realize how great is the hope to which he is calling you—the magnificence and splendor of the inheritance promised to Christians—and how tremendous is the power available to us who believe in God. That power is the same divine energy which was demonstrated in Christ when he raised him from the dead and gave him the place of supreme honor in Heaven—a place that is infinitely superior to any conceivable command, authority, power or control, and which carries with it a name far beyond any name that could ever be used in this world or the world to come."

WOW! I didn't start to copy Phillips translation, but God knows what he is doing. I feel "tingly" all over from the magnitude of the power of God in our present, right-now lives and how we are dealing with "hydrogen energy" when we turn God loose to use our lives. Here it is not even 7:00 in the morning and thrills are already permeating my whole being. This is Sunday and He always "outdoes" himself on Sunday, so I hope I can contain it all; or rather, let it all flow through me into the people God is preparing to receive it today. Bet they are already excited too, even though they don't know what's in store for them.

I lay awake about an hour around 3:00 or 4:00 this morning because when I communicate with you, and more especially when you related just a few of the thrills of the great things you had experienced on this trip, I just don't have the "calm" of sleep, but it seems God gives energies without sleep! One thought that passed through (or into—it's still there) my mind was what an earthshaking or people-soul-shaking thing would happen if our feeling of this tremendous excitement could be transmitted to others by the AP or UP carrying worldwide a daily letter which simply started "Dear Frances" or "Dear Charles" and be a front page, two-column-wide letter just relating these exciting things and feelings. The thought of its effect in offsetting the negative front pages of all newspapers is awesome—if it were really transferred to others the way we feel. But God is the only one who could transmit the very thrilling excitement because he also operates the receiving minds of whatever he says through us! Now,

I don't feel I'm that kind of a writer, but I have absolutely no doubt that God and Christ's Holy Spirit can write whatever would be right just like He wrote "God Is Fabulous," because He really is fabulous.

I must stop to get ready to go hear the Youth Choir (now 154 Plus) at the early church service. I get those "spiritual goose-pimples" when I see and hear them open their hearts in exuberant song to God because I dearly love them. How I would love to relate just one of your or my experiences that happened that week (God is "NOW") each Sunday morning just before they sing.

> Turn Loose—I love you in Christ,
> Charles

P.S. Enclosed is a little check to make sure you don't ever hesitate to call me from anywhere at any time because long-distance and long conversations cost money. God has plenty of ways to supply your daily needs, and I'm ready to be one of his ways.

* * *

November 3, 1969

Dear Charles:

If you see Cloud 9 floating by, don't grab me off, but grab this letter, because that's exactly where I am right now—on that good old Cloud 9.

Tonight is our church's Living File night for calling and sometimes I think I must be a rebel of sorts, because I just can't go out on the little pink siips they give me, so I just "hang loose with Jesus" to see what happens. Tonight I was led to the home of a woman in my Sunday School class who has been absent for two Sundays because of the illness of her children but who had previously asked me to visit her husband who is a real nasty thing. I asked God to prepare his heart, and when we got there he was sleeping, and got woke up out of a sound sleep, but God had done such a fabulous job, he prayed to receive Christ with no static on his part at all. It was so thrilling to see how God's Holy Spirit moved in on the situation. I had taken a woman with me who is a new Christian, but an exciting one, but who has a tendency to talk too much and so tonight I just looked over and said, "Shhhhhhhhh." She really got the message in a hurry, and didn't open her mouth and interrupt God's Holy Spirit again. I love to go on calls with people who are sensitive to the leading of God's Holy Spirit, but it kills me to go with someone who keeps on blabbing, ignoring the nudges of God's Holy Spirit.

Your letter just thrilled me to death when it arrived this morning. I was so shocked that it arrived so quickly. I had wanted to write you yesterday, but the alternator in my new car went pfft (Praise the Lord anyway) and so my daughter and I were slightly on foot yesterday or dependent on other people, so I couldn't get to the office to type you a letter, and believe me when I say you'd never be able to read my handwriting. (I can't even read it myself.)

I enjoyed your quote from the Phillips translation. I'm doing some rereading in that translation preparing for Wednesday night's service, which I'm in charge of since my pastor is away. One of the things I'm emphasizing is the power and the joy which accompanies the infilling of the Holy Spirit. And your quote from Ephesians was great!

Just reading your letters "grabs" me. I often wonder what it is that makes some people find the real joy in Christ where so many people never ever seem to find it. And I just thrill right along with you because I can sense exactly what you are experiencing. And like you, wouldn't it be fabulous to be able to transmit this to others via AP or UP. I had to laugh at your comments concerning your ability as a writer. I think you do a fabulous job, because you really communicate exactly how you feel and to my way of thinking this is the entire secret. But then we both know it's when God is using us that His ability to communicate can be manifested perfectly in whatever comes out.

I'm enclosing a schedule of where I'm going to be the next week. You'd better pray for the ministers up that way . . . and then be praying that God will allow me to challenge them as they have never been challenged.

I covet your prayers, Charles, concerning my office. Today my son hired the last person we needed to replace me in the office, so as of Wednesday of this week, there will be no responsibilities that are mine. Praise the Lord! In my heart there was a little temporary flip-flopping, because it's hard to turn your back on everything you've worked so hard for, but I know that it's God's perfect will for this to happen, and I know that He will supply my every need. And then to back this up further, your letter came with the check, and believe it or not, another check came from a pastor of a church asking me to use the money to extend the "unique" ministry I have. He said he thought I was "high octane." He wasn't in his church when I spoke there, but he said he had heard how the Lord had used "this gal." Fabulous things are happening in the office where Tom is concerned and I am continually praying that the Lord will give me the know-how to let Him handle the entire situation. So far I've had to bite my lip a couple of times, but because I believe with my heart and soul that He has spoken, it has really been a lot easier than I ever anticipated. And would you believe there has never been a moment's doubt as to whether or not I was doing the right thing?

Another book is welling up within me—God always seems to let me know when I should allow time for writing, so possibly book No. 4, which might just be titled "Hang Loose With Jesus," will be written before long. And better be careful what you write in letters, because you never know what might appear in print when you write to me! The one quote I am going to use is the one about "exploding," and depending on the Lord to put you back together again. Loved that one.

Thank you so much for giving up your early morning sleep to write to me. My heart sang as I felt the contagious spirit of your excitement as you have been sharing Christ.

May God continue to pour out His Spirit upon you, and may you continue to be a blessing to others.

In His great love,
Frances

P.S. I'm just going to pass on a scripture which was sent to me right after *God Is Fabulous* was published. (Which translation do you read the most? I think we all have a favorite. Mine happens to be the

22

Revised Standard.) I Peter 1: 23-25: "You have been born anew, not of perishable seed, *but of imperishable,* through the living and abiding word of God; for 'All flesh is like grass, and all its glory like the flowers of grass. The grass withers, and the flower falls, But the word of the Lord abides forever.' That word is the good news which was preached to you."

I never come across that scripture but what I revel again in the knowledge that I have been born anew of imperishable seed. Praise the Lord!

November 5, 1969

Dear Charles:

Just a real quick note. I was listening to Doug Oldham this morning as I was getting dressed—his records really thrill me, and I was really getting charged up for the day, and happened to see something I thought you might get a kick out of. I had a few of these napkins left over from some tea or something, so thought you might like to have one of each kind. (Napkins with words "God is Fabulous" printed on them.) Think I'll have some of these printed up for the New Year's Eve Party.

And here's a little booklet ("Live in His Presence," Charles Weber) I've enjoyed very much. I've never met Mr. Weber, but I'm sure you have. I wrote him and told him he ought to have a new picture made because he looks like a crab, but he must not feel like one inside if he really believes the little book he wrote. I think it's a good little tract, and I use it a lot with new Christians.

Wrote a lot of letters last night for my California trip next year—I had about 75 letters requesting speaking dates, but I sure can't fill them all. Got a real exciting call last night about a Miami date to a church where I had just been in September. I'm speaking tomorrow night (Thursday) to an Evangelical Church before I leave town on Saturday to really try and supercharge some ministers.

You'd probably have hysterics if I told you my first reaction to the check you sent me, but then the Lord really got in touch with me and reminded me of your kind and generous heart. And I'll surprise you and call you one of these nights again soon.

Drop me a line, and keep me in your prayers, especially when I travel. I need God's grace to keep me strong, full of energy, and lots of spiritual vitamins so I won't catch a cold in the weather I'm not used to being in, although this morning in Miami it's 53 and delightful!

Drop me a line, or maybe even more than just one line.

He lives!

Frances

P.S. I'm praying the Lord will enable you to do your accounting work much more rapidly than ever before, so you can spend time on God's Squad.

* * *

Houston, Texas, November 6, 1969 (11:15 P.M.)

Dearest Frances,

All day today I attended a tax seminar which was well presented and very essential to the tax practitioner, but to gain attention the only way they seem to know is to tell shady stories. How sad.

And then—God blasted me out of that world when I got home with your letter that thrilled me even before opening it, and then inside it was such a vast difference from the rest of the day. How I love that difference!!

Now, I didn't plan to answer until something very exciting happened—I got your letter about 6:00 P.M.—it's now 11:00 P.M. same nite and some fabulous *things* have happened!! God doesn't wait long to give joy more than we can imagine. (And before I forget again, please don't feel you need to take time to answer all my letters—just let Him use you in this most vital witnessing you are doing; except when he tells you to write me. Of course, I wish that was every day, but just an occasional letter will be wonderful. *I know God has a very definite purpose in your entering my life and I'm very glad and will stand by, ready to run for him when he says go! Man, I'll Go!)*

Events of the nite:

1. I took the liberty to read a big part of your letter to Mrs. Bevis, my mother-in-law. She thinks the world of you and your mission. Your letter gave her a boost.

2. I called my brother Milton near Corpus to visit for a few minutes. He and his wife Mary have been richly impressed with the way God has shielded me from grief and loneliness and in its place has given the most marvelous joy I have ever known—and I really tell them about it—some of my other family members too. They will someday know God better.

3. I called new church members for interest in the choir and out of about four or five calls, one will be in the choir—a young married lady. This seems to be God's way—he gets me with one or two or a few at a time, but the composite is already being felt at the church. I'm anxious, but am just being completely available and God does everything.

4. A friend called—I had witnessed over an hour to him a month or so ago and God nudged him again tonite. He is *bored* with church, and I guess I would be too if God wasn't alive in me!

5. I read for about an hour—partly in Ian Thomas' book *The Saving Life of Christ* and partly in the Bible. This book is great for telling how you are out in a dry wilderness until Jesus Christ through the Holy Spirit lives in you when you are totally surrendered and that nothing else will do but complete bankruptcy of yourself and becoming rich in Christ. He will be here a week from Saturday to speak at a Youth for Christ meeting and I hope God gets a carload ready to go with me, and I expect he will!

Incidentally, I read the Revised Standard for about a thousand hours (literally) during Jeanne's illness, mostly in the New Testament and love it. I am now just about through the New Testament in Phillips and in some ways like it even better, but use both together.

6. Now for the fabulous reason I'm writing this letter, which may be finished by midnight—

After all the above events, the reading best of all, I felt God's Holy Spirit very close. I always kneel at my bedside and pray aloud even though no human ear is listening, and while I was praying for you,

Tom and your need, I just bubbled over. I feel like you are about to turn all the way loose and when you do, the business and Tom will be saved (and you don't like that word, but it fits here). I know you have faith abundant to turn everything loose to God, but you seem yet a little concerned. I know God will still use you in the business when he wants you there.

While I was praying I started talking to God about how I thanked him for doing so many thrilling things when I just had this tiny little faith (which he gave). Suddenly His Holy Spirit said that he never needs big faith—really he doesn't ask for it—just the little mustard-seed size. I was overjoyed because I have always prayed for more faith. I don't know if the thought is communicating or not, but I received a whole release from searching for "more faith" and know now he can do anything he plans through me with no more faith than I now have. It's God through Christ who takes over immediately when the spark of faith ignites and his power is all the power it takes for the work he has been doing through me, through you, through many others. This marvelous message is why I got off my knees to write this. You know how I have known to turn loose, and have, in full surrender, but to suddenly have all the faith I'll need the rest of my life is wonderful—just the little bit is God's plenty!

And the clock just struck midnight.

God has been his usual fabulous self in giving you absolute assurance you are doing exactly the right thing in your business.

Oh, yes, you will get a bang out of this. A secretary I'm acquainted with has been reading *God is Fabulous* and the Holy Spirit has been telling her a lot of the thrilling things happening to me—using my voice; she said it was hard to believe, and I told her she need have no doubt; that all in the book is exactly true. She said, "Well, I really believe it's all true—I just can't believe it all happens so fast!!" Isn't that great—she then said, "I've tried to quit smoking and know how hard it is and for you to just instantly quit by turning it over to God."

I'm so anxious for you to get started on No. 4 book—you should do it in twenty-five hours since you are experienced—it's terrific when God dictates that fast to you.

I will wish to be able to read the manuscript by the end of the year. *I feel God has said OK for me to be there for your New Year's Eve PTL* (was that the name—"Party for the Lord"?). *I'm excited about it and the only one that will be able to change my plans will be God, so if he doesn't say no, I'll be in touch.* Now, how can I sleep tonite with so much excitement—the more I think about your books the more anxious I get to have them. I've given out about forty each of No. 1 and No. 2 except for about ten I was paid for—this is really a joy and it is the extra tool that exactly parallels the things I tell people about the very "living, exciting God"—and more are believing and longing for a touch of it—so God will soon have others in my church "turning loose."

PTL IN ALL CAPS!!!!!

Yes, being born anew in the very Spirit of Christ truly is fabulous, so as I float by on Cloud #8 I will

28

wave goodnite to a delightfully loving friend who rides Cloud #9 most of the time.

With abounding love in Christ,
Charles

I'll be praying with you as you fill your schedule.

TURN LOOSE   TURN LOOSE   TURN LOOSE

*   *   *

November 8th, 1969
(Just before plane time)

Dear Charles:

Even though I'm racing around madly to catch my plane, just had to write a few lines to let you know I only scanned through your letter very quickly—almost didn't open it—almost decided to save it for the plane trip, but couldn't stand it, so I just tore it open and really "speed read" it, and it just grabbed me.

Haven't got time to write more, but I'm so excited about my trip and really anticipating the plane trip so I can really enjoy every single word you wrote. I tucked the other letters in my suitcase so I can reread them, too.

I'll be praying for you—and if you'll remember at 11:00 P.M. your time, I'll be praying at midnight where I am and we'll let our prayers join together, shall we?

Remember—11:00 for you—and midnight for me.

Am excitedly looking forward to New Year's Eve. Please pray for all kinds of miracles.

In His exciting steps,
Frances

No more time or I'll miss the plane.

En Route—on tour—November 12, 1969

Dear Charles:

Please pardon the stationery because I addressed envelopes to you before I left home, but forgot to bring stationery, so borrowed this.

Wish I had a typewriter—I would write you pages and pages—this trip has really given me some experiences! Some fabulous—and some not so fabulous!

I spoke at a ministerial session yesterday, and the response was fantastic. I spoke on personal soul winning and on letting the power of God's Holy Spirit do the job in all areas, and I pray that I really challenged them to go out and be personal soul winners!

At the end of the service an old-timer who was sitting on the front row walked up to the pulpit and pointed his finger at me and said, "Take off those earrings so God can use you!"

Charles, I almost fainted! He sounded like he was accusing me of adultery or something! I was absolutely rooted to the spot. I thought surely I couldn't have heard correctly! But I did. The tension in the air was fantastic. All of a sudden I said, "Praise the Lord!" And then added, "In case you're interested, I serve God, and no man. Until God tells me to take them off, I'll leave them on." I thought the meeting was going to end in a riot because every pastor jumped to my rescue (P.T.L.). (They tell me the man does this kind of stuff all the time.) Praise the Lord, I had put on the whole armor of God. While some of this was going on, I slipped down to the altar and knelt down to pray to ask God to really intervene and stop the nonsense. You'd better believe that my heart was really pounding!

The ministers really came to the altar and the whole meeting ended on a real glorious note.

The service tonight was great—about 50 came to the altar. Three of the boys on the No. 1 basketball squad accepted Christ. Then at the last minute I felt led to have a soul winning class—so after the church service we had a class, and 41 people stayed to learn how to win souls.

I'm pooped—will try and write more in the A.M. In the meantime, it's 12:00 midnight, so it's time to pray!

Here it is early Thursday morning. Woke up saying, "Praise the Lord—what fabulous things are we going to do?" and you know I have a real tremendous feeling something really exciting is going to happen. As a matter of fact, I woke up real early this morning. It seemed like God's Holy Spirit nudged me —probably so the Lord and I could have some fellowship early in the morning—then naturally I thought about you and wondered if maybe some pastor today would tell me there was a letter waiting for me.

The Lord really made an inroad into a factory in this area. Can't wait to share with you how a girl on the production line (she tests automatic timers) prayed to receive Christ as the "reject lights" were flashing on and off. It was really exciting when I thought I was going to end up in jail because the plant superintendent put his hand on my shoulder and said, "What are you doing here!!!!" Oh, well, Paul and Silas and Frances!!

Time is flying and I've got to get dressed to go to a radio station. Keep on praying, and please remember to pray that God will keep me from catching a cold or the flu—seems like the flu bug is really up here, but I'm depending on God to keep me well.

I'll be home Tuesday instead of Monday—don't know what time yet, but if it's not too late and you have a letter waiting for me—I might give you a ring.

My spirit joins yours in prayer.

In His exciting service,
Frances

* * *

AUTHOR'S NOTE: While on this tour I realized that I had begun to think more and more about Charles Hunter and more and more I had a desire to share everything with him that happened on the tour, and it seemed every time I changed planes in an airport I found myself looking for a little card to send him, just to let him know I was thinking about him. More and more I had begun to look for the letters with the beautiful handwriting, through which the love of God flowed in tremendous quantities, and all of a sudden I began to be concerned about myself.

I KNEW beyond a shadow of doubt that God had placed a special call upon my life and I felt there was no time in my life for love or romance or anything like that, but nevertheless every time I thought about Christ (which was and is constantly) I thought about Charles, and vice versa. I finally decided that because I was spending so much time writing to Charles, talking to Charles via long-distance telephone calls, and spending so much time thinking about him, that the devil himself had sent this charming man to get my mind off of the things of God! And there was a period of time when I felt that Charles was the devil himself!

Somehow or other as I faced this situation square-ly, I wondered how he could be of the devil because we never discussed anything except the exciting things that Christ was doing in both of our lives, and yet I felt that anything that took up as much of my time as my thoughts of Charles must be of the devil, so I did what I always do when I'm not sure of God's will—I put out the fleece.

I had prayerfully considered all the things con-cerning Charles, and I knew that my human heart was wanting to share every single little thought and every single miracle with Charles, and I suppose I realized that my human heart was falling in love with him, but I also knew that if Charles were of the devil I would never be happy with him, so I made a deci-sion to ask God to answer the fleece, and after some of the greatest anguish I have ever known, I put out the following fleece: I said, "God, if Charles IS NOT OF YOU, LET HIM FALL IN LOVE WITH SOMEONE ELSE BEFORE HE COMES TO MIAMI."And then I cried all night. I knew that I wanted Charles, but I also knew that if Charles were not of God I didn't want him. So I not only asked God to let me know definitely by answering the fleece, but I also asked one tiny little favor—to not let my heart be broken if Charles were not of Him.

Peculiarly, as much as I felt drawn to Charles, I

knew I had to be obedient to what God wanted out of my life. As with Abraham of old who had to be willing to lay his son on the altar for God, I had to be willing to lay Charles on the altar of sacrifice for God and yet God didn't demand that I give him up, he only demanded that I be willing to.

What happened next turned out to be hysterical at times. All of a sudden Charles became the most sought-after bachelor in Houston. He was flooded with invitations to dinner parties and functions of various natures, but to make things more interesting, all of these invitations were from very attractive women . . . all the right age . . . and all very eligible!

Charles has often said that most people think of God as a somber judge waiting up there to clamp down on us, but it's delightful to know that God has a fabulous sense of humor, too, and the next several weeks were most interesting as I watched how God was handling this fleece. Of course, Charles knew nothing about the fleece that I had put out, and he was bewildered by all this sudden attention. He told me all of these women were women with spiritual problems who had seen the great change in his life and who wanted this same excitement. (After we were married, I told him that women are sneaky!) Interestingly enough, each of the women involved were given copies of my books, and Charles had to cut each "date" short because he told them he called me nightly when I was home at 11 o'clock Houston time, or midnight Miami time.

*   *   *

34

Houston, Texas 77024
November 15, 1969

Dear Fran, Paul and Silas!

Don't know how you did it, but you really showered me with exciting letters all week in spite of your travels and no doubt very long hours of talking. I kinda felt something was missing because to answer your letters seems to "keep in touch" but I felt I shouldn't try to reach you without full addresses. All week long I have wanted to write, so tonite I'll try to make up for it and take this to the Post Office so you, I hope, will have it when you get home.

This last week has been two great weeks (try to add that one!)—one for you and one for me and two for God! That really adds to four, doesn't it?

You can be sure each nite at 11:00 my time I was praying for you and knew you would always be talking to God at midnight. You just can't expect anything except fabulous days and nights when you are constantly in close conversation with him. I really stay excited because of the magnitude of power managing our lives and I hope it becomes more meaningful to others for *total* surrender.

One page down and ———— to go! Something seems to be about ready to burst out and I hardly know what *not* to tell first or how much *not* to tell; wish we could just be together for about forty hours to relate details of events—that should be about enough time to tell a couple weeks of experiences.

Just happened to see the back of one of your home-typed letters—the little P.S. about your prayer to speed up my accounting so I can spend more time on God's Squad. I'm really for that, but I know he is arranging for whatever he has in mind and it will be a lot more exciting than accounting; although I do enjoy that also. He is using a great amount of my time now talking to clients about himself. That reminds me of one of this week's fabulous encounters (wish I could tell you details of all of them but I couldn't finish before I would be behind again —they really happen fast!). Let's see, how far back do I start with this.

A lady who is a private secretary for a large industrial concern (client of mine) has been a very pleasant person to work with, but now she is an excited person who really wants to get some of these thrilling times in her life. I'm not sure but I think she is divorced . . . or maybe she is a widow with 3 children. Sometime I will ask her if we stop talking about God long enough. Anyway, I'll move the story back to Jeanne's funeral in May, which was an unusually great experience for about three hundred people, including the pastor, and certainly including me, because God really made close contact with a variety of people. It's not often that someone can work for God in a fantastic way right through their own funeral, but Jeanne's life kept going because Christ was so much in her spirit; his love and light reached right into a lot of lives, including the lady (June) I'm telling about. I had told her about many of the things God did in our lives during Jeanne's illness, including the miracles of Christ speaking audibly to me this one time; being lifted into Christ's presence and the Holy Spirit telling me three times "Charles, let me do this my way" and then Jeanne's physical healing for the short but wonderful period of time.

June went to the funeral, along with quite a few of the top officials of the company she works for. She just related more details to me this week about what an impact the demonstration of God's sufficient care over me during the funeral had on them. She said they were discussing it again the other day and were amazed at the absence of grief and the presence of God's life in mine. This is thrilling because it has influenced most of the lives in this business enterprise from the chairman of the board, president, vice-president, secretaries and clerks, and that's a long terrific story. I didn't mean to get into that part of my life, but June's life was deeply moved by the pastor's enthusiastic message because he "had something he really was anxious to say about Jeanne" and he said it right.

I had promised June a copy of *God Is Fabulous* and *Go, Man, Go* a couple of weeks ago, but got side-tracked and gave them to the secretary of another company, so she got the only two copies I had with me (and that's another exciting story which God is rapidly unfolding). Anyway, I finished a job last Monday—I think it was Monday, in this building at five minutes till five and had just enough time to drop the books into June's hands. Well, five minutes in God's hands turned into an hour and five minutes. June and I left her office at 6:00. She wanted to hear more of the excitement in our lives and sometimes when I get to talking it's about as much of your exciting life as my experiences, so God surely must have had a good reason for you to charge into my life. She is longing so for God to control her life and he is changing it and she is thrilled. I talked to her again Thursday (no, it was Friday—yesterday) and she said she read both books the night I gave them to her and was rereading *God is Fabulous* and finds a marvelous thrill in the way God is working.

I had invited her to hear Major Ian Thomas speak in Pasadena at a Baptist Church. I heard him at three services and sat next to him after a luncheon while he talked informally to about 25 of us. He is a man about 55 years of age, from England (maybe you know him) who asked Christ to be his Saviour at age 12 and worked himself almost to exhaustion by age 19 (for God) and when he was about ready to give up, he learned the great secret you and I have had revealed to us: let God do everything while we are totally available to him, *resting* in the absolute assurance he will do a magnificent job if we will let him. For 40 years he has felt this great thrill you feast on daily (milk and honey instead of manna), this living Christ living in our spirits. He has traveled over 60 countries—the most marvelous preacher I have ever heard ('cause you aren't a preacher, you say!). I asked him if in his travels and worldwide speaking engagements he finds many who let God act daily for them and he said very few.

Well, back to June: She said she had been having quite a number of problems that left her rather discouraged and that she was amazed that several times while she was in a low mood, the phone would ring and I would be on the other end with just the thrilling attitude she needed at the time. I thank God constantly for the joyful mission he has given me up to now. I don't know what he plans for my life yet, but he sure makes the approach to it interesting! It's also interesting to see how much alike and yet how much difference He has given your mission and mine (mine so far). You "enthuse" people and cause masses to accept Christ. I enthuse people and constantly press for nothing short of TOTAL commitment of their lives. Maybe he wants me to follow along after you and talk further to those seed which fall on good, rich ground and their lives flourish. This I fully know—he will beautifully "do it his way" because we both know we are only available with absolutely no power or ability of our own. I sure wandered around telling you about June, but guess all these thoughts are moulded into what God is doing for her.

You have had several things that "grab" you, but you almost had two people "grab" you this time. The "old-timer" is so typical of the millions of church specialists who try so hard to be sure of some theological interpretation or some "no—no" that they lose sight of the very simple good news of Christ living in us. It really is sad. You just must reread in Phillips translation about this "no—no" religion—Letter to Colossae—2:16 to end of chapter. Bless your heart, I'll bet you were scared again when the factory foreman laid his hand on you, but you really don't need to fear because God also laid his hand on you—and his hand is the most powerful of all.

I read part of your letter from Huntington to a young man today and he really thought it fabulous to be a part of your action. He also liked your return address—and I do too! AT LARGE!!! P.T.L. Great! I get a kick out of reading your handwriting and do very well with it—don't let that slow you down—I just enjoy them longer when I sometimes stop to figure out a word. Really, you do quite well. I liked the fact that three of the No. 1 basketball players gave their hearts to Christ.

Boy, I must stop—nine pages already—I also wrote several hours today—continuation of writing about the fantastic miracles in Jeanne's and my life—it's getting rather lengthy. If I ever finish I'll send you a copy. I started with one thought in mind of sending it to three families who don't know Jeanne died (two in England), but it also is partially in response to several people asking me to write the experiences I have been talking about.

Please order a new pair of glasses or stop me from writing such long letters.

Power - Terrific - Love
and God really is fabulous,
Charles

My prayers continue.

*　*　*

November 18, 1969—fogged in airport

Charles, dear:

All I can say is P.T.L.A.—Praise the Lord Anyway. I'm at the airport waiting. They have canceled all the flights because of fog in Chicago, but are hoping the field will clear by 10:00 P.M. It's now 6:30. The planes are stacked up in Chicago for a 3-hour delay and they aren't stacking up any more. So P.T.L.A.—it gives me a chance to write to you.

Really had a fabulous day yesterday—five services. You'd better believe I stayed awake only to be able to pray at midnight with you. I was really exhausted because the altar services were tremendous —but when I'm on my knees for such a long time and involved emotionally it really drains the power out of me—the services were great, though, and the power of God was unbelievable.

I'm enclosing a copy of a newspaper article by a newswoman who interviewed me. She wasn't a Christian when we met, but somehow it looks as though she got the message from the tone of her article. How do you like the headline "Granny Go-Go is B.A. (Born Again)"?

I was on the radio today—and the fellow called back today and said, "Praise the Lord—this is W.B."—and we almost cracked up.

Then I spoke at the Lions Club—WOW. What a bunch of sinners! I only had a short time, but when I told my cigarette story all the men almost choked on their cigars and cigarettes but no one lit another cigarette after I told the story of how the Lord delivered me from cigarettes. The pastor almost croaked when I told them that most of them were probably going to hell! That's sure an unladylike word, but so effective and so necessary where certain types of people are concerned. It seems that many times in an organization like that they have to have "hell" scared out of them because they don't seem anxious to respond to God's love.

Well, how 'bout this. They just canceled the 10 P.M. flight—so here I am stuck for the night. No trains run until noon tomorrow—but P.T.L.A.

Better go make some telephone calls and arrangements. Joan called me tonight and said there was a big envelope from you. Can't wait to get home and read your thoughts and find out all the exciting things you've been doing.

You're in my thoughts constantly and also in my prayers. Wish you were sitting right here so we could have a good old prayer meeting!

In His great and exciting love,
Frances

(Letter written on back of fliers describing services in town just leaving.)

*　　*　　*

AUTHOR'S NOTE: This is when the telephone calls started in earnest. Upon returning from this tour, I phoned Charles to share the excitement of the trip with him, and then a series of almost nightly telephone calls began.

*　　*　　*

Houston, Texas, November 20, 1969 (A.M.)

Dearest Fran,

It's past time to go to work and I have a busy day —unless He decides I do something else and then work really doesn't matter!

I was looking for a magnificent scripture I wanted to tell you about and haven't found it yet, but in the process read Philippians 3:4-14 in Phillips—WOW!! Total surrender in bold print! And then the last sentence in 1:23b of Letter to Colossae—it really tells the heart of the great secret. And again Romans 3:27 tells where we personally stand in our achievements, and add II Corinthians 4:7.

Well, PTLA! I didn't find what *I* was looking for,

but maybe *God* spotted for me what He wanted.

Must run, but will try to get home earlier tonite and write more.

What a wonderful 40 minutes by phone Tuesday nite! Don't do it again unless you want God to do some really fantastic things because he has a genuine purpose in all this! Just to be able to contain the joy I have is almost more than this ol' house can hold, but when I feel your joy along with it, it's tremendous!

Bye now.
Christ loves you,
Charles

P.S. Please don't catch the 4:29.

*   *   *

Thursday nite
November 20, 1969 10:20

Dearest Fran,

Love your return addresses! Received your letter from the fogged airport "FEG STRANDED!!!! P.T.L.A." So many people are stranded because they are fogged in spiritually.

I was really getting excited about a new Christmas development but got it squashed. We have our Christmas choir Oratorio Sunday nite, Dec. 21st, and I just shouldn't consider missing this. Well, I talked to my brother Clyde and his wife Lee in Alabama tonite to start New Year's Party plans. They excited me with news that you will be there Saturday the 20th for a youth rally and on Sunday, so I was ready to be there also. It would have been fun, but unless God changes my program (and you never know when he will) I will probably get to Alabama early Monday morning to ride with them to Miami via St. Pete for extra visit time, or I can fly to Miami Monday morning, depending on your plans. You can be very sure I'll be where God wants me when he wants me there, so if you get a nudge before I do, speak up.

I got a call from June today and asked how she was doing, and she answered with real excitement in her voice, "Great!" She is really turning her life over to Christ in a big way—it's wonderful.

This morning I worked downtown again for the fourth day in one office and it sure would surprise me if God let me stay in one place that long without getting someone stirred up, so two more ladies know a little about what it means to get excited for God! One is rather crippled with arthritis—tears just about opened up when I was telling some of the fabulous things God does every day. The other person is about 30, a very personable and attractive lady, who will probably visit my church Sunday morning. I don't know what God has in mind for her, but from the moment I met her a couple of months ago I felt spiritually at ease with her. I can see a longing in her eyes for some of this tremendous feeling of Christ living IN us. She has both of your books (also the other lady). Someday I'll tell you the next chapter in her life—when God produces it! Also today I had lunch with an architect client and a city councilman—sure they heard of the fantastic events taking place.

Sure liked your stationery from Decatur—that was a great presentation of your—can't think of the right word, but anyway I've amended that flier they put out so it reads: "America's Most Exciting Woman."

Hope you are rested by now. You really had it rough physically, but smooth spiritually.

I attended a choir officers' meeting tonite and it was nice, but is sure hard for me to hold a genuine interest when all the activities planned fall so short of the marvelous joy God offers us. P.T.L.A.

Bedtime—tomorrow nite and Saturday nite "Football for the Lord"—and you can be sure God will be "on the ball" for the ones I'll be with—he never misses!

In His mighty love,
Charles
TURN LOOSE!

TURN LOOSE!

*   *   *

Miami, Florida, November 20, 1969 P.M.

Dear Charles:

Just a real quickie note tonight just to let you know I'm thinking about you and anticipating the holiday season. Christmas is so completely different as a Christian, isn't it? I remember the Christmases of years ago and then I compare them with today, and there sure isn't any comparison. I also think of Thanksgiving and how completely different I feel on Thanksgiving than I did 5 years ago.

Would you believe that for the last 4 years I have had a bologna sandwich for my Thanksgiving dinner? We have our State Youth Convention each year over Thanksgiving and so Joan and I are always on the road and instead of the usual turkey, we have a bologna sandwich. But what "milk and honey," as

45

you put it, a bologna sandwich is when you're traveling for the cause of Jesus Christ.

Did I tell you about last Thanksgiving? The problem with my leg was so acute I was scheduled to go into the hospital on Thursday morning, which meant I had to cancel out on speaking at the Youth Convention. I was in such pain I was almost ready to have my leg cut off (and I have a tremendously high pain tolerance). My doctor came by the house and said they'd have to put me in for at least 2 or 3 weeks, and I was in such agony I agreed. But . . . I called my pastor and asked him to come over and pray. He brought two other ministers with him, and they stood at the foot of my bed, and instead of laying hands on my head, he grabbed my big toe and then prayed that God would heal my leg so that I could go to the convention the next day. Then my doctor called me at 6:00 the next morning and said at midnight he had been compelled to crawl out of bed (he's my spiritual child in case you're interested) and go down on his knees and ask God to keep me out of the hospital. His anguished plea was, "God, I just don't believe you want her in the hospital." He asked me how the fever in my leg was. Would you believe (of course you would) the fever and pain was gone from my leg and I have never again had fever and pain! Immediately I asked him if I could go to the Youth Convention and he went through the ceiling, but finally he said if they gave me a private room I could go. Well, you know how youth conventions are—you get in a room with 30 other kids and WOW! Joan had already gone ahead to the convention and she called me back to tell me that she didn't know how come I rated a private room, but I sure had one. I said, "P.T.L.," got out of bed and went to the Convention. I have a feeling that's one convention I'll never forget. Fortunately for me it was in Ft. Lauderdale, so it was close and I didn't have far to drive. This year it's at the Jack Tar Hotel in Clearwater. Again I have the witnessing conference this year and I'm excited! We'll be driving over on Thursday morning and will come back Saturday night.

It's an interesting thing, but I feel the problem with my legs is going to be answered in the overall plan God has been revealing. Now that I'm not tied down to this dumb office, my legs have been swelling only a minute amount, and do you remember how swollen they were in Houston? I have a feeling the Lord's been telling me for the last couple of years to knock off working so hard and I just wouldn't listen, but I think it's so exciting to see how He's so completely prepared my heart so that there is absolutely no sorrow or unhappiness at leaving this business. I haven't taken a penny's worth of salary since last September. It just seems that God has said He'll provide every need, and my speaking tours have more than provided for Joan and me.

I just got a long-distance call asking me to speak to the ministers of the State of Florida in February. And by the way, I have a feeling I'll be at your brother's church in December (just the week before Christmas). Well, how about this. I just discovered that I'm going to be in Bessemer, Alabama with Clarence Dillon and some of the other pastors, and I looked in the yearbook, and unless I'm NUTS, your brother is in Bessemer. Well, that might be a good time for you to spend with him and then we'll give him a double-barreled effect. Or maybe you can follow up right behind me and then we know his church won't have a chance.

Well, I'd better scoot home because I promised Tom I'd work tomorrow too, and I've got to get to bed early so I can write the final chapter on *Hot Line to Heaven* . . . and you know the most amazing thing? I always "Hang Loose with Jesus" as you know and it was only today that God actually revealed exactly how He wanted the final chapter. It's a good thing I don't panic, because my publisher has the rest of the book and gave me until this weekend to complete it, and I didn't know until today how the Lord wanted it completed. But I never worried, because I remembered that He has never let me down.

I'm going to start "Hang Loose with Jesus" right away. And by the way, did you understand me when I said I read part of your letter in a church. And talking about your thoughts, you might store up some little gems concerning "Hanging Loose," and how you learned the secret; I might just incorporate them in my book.

And did you know that my book *Hot Line to Heaven* is dedicated to my son? I think it's amazing that somehow the Lord revealed to me a long time ago that this was the book for Tom. As you know, *Go, Man, Go* is dedicated to Joan. And the first one, of course, to the "men in my life." Doesn't that make it sound interesting? It always grabs people when they realize that the first one is Jesus Christ.

Enough for now—my thoughts and prayers are with you, and I can sense your undergirding prayers for me. May God continue to bless you and keep you in His great love and in His perfect plan for your life.

I'll be counting the days until I see you so we can share all this excitement without having to pound it out on a typewriter. (But aren't you glad it's type-written instead of longhand?)

In His exciting steps and fabulous love,

Frances

He lives!

*   *   *

November 21, 1969—Miami, Florida

Dear Charles:

I was so wound up after talking to you last night, that I couldn't go to sleep even though I was ex-hausted. It's so great being able to just share the blessings of God which everyone could have if they would just believe!

I'm so thrilled to see how the Lord is using you, and I'm so thrilled to think about all the exciting people I want to meet you when you're over here. I'm also going to try and see if we can't get you to some Campus Crusade excitement while you're here because I think this would be fabulous for you. I really believe that Campus Crusade for Christ has been one of the greatest influences in my life and they are really responsible for the excitement of Christ in my life.

My pastor came in today and he's so glad I'm back. One of the women in the church called and said the church just isn't the same when I'm not here. I told her to stop that nonsense or I'd stop being humble.

Give me a few little hints, will you? I want to write a very short booklet to give to new Christians to help them grow in their Christian life. What do you think created the greatest spurt in your Christian growth? Was it Bible reading, was it learning how to pray, was it beginning to pray more, was it understanding God's Holy Spirit, was it learning to let God work through you, or what? I have my own ideas on this but I want to incorporate ideas from other individuals if possible. I think there is a great need in this area for just the RIGHT kind of booklet.

More tomorrow.

In His exciting love,

Frances

P.S. Got a letter from Bill Menefee and he said he's told over a hundred people how we got him out of bed just to share Christian love!

* * *

Houston, Texas
Sunday, November 23, 1969
8 A.M.

Fran, PTL—Bang!

I think I just exploded! What a fantastic week!!

Where do I start? So many wonderful things going at one time and all so very thrilling and exciting. Guess I'll start with last nite's "Football for Christ." It's even an extra gift that God gives to give us a very thrilling life of entertainment as part of his bountiful spiritual gifts!! (Prissy, one of my cats, is laying upside down on the desk talking in cat language to me and trying to out-rank you for attention.) But I don't believe anything except God's

50

activities (other than letters to you) can have much priority in my life right now.

Fran, it's real interesting and getting more so just to wonder what God has in his plans for us. It is astounding to realize (and I can hardly realize it) that as far apart as our lives have been—strangers except for about a month—our lives are so closely involved in something very mysterious but so very, very certain that it all is being done only by God and there is absolutely nothing either of us can do to change it because our lives are totally God's; that his supernatural-natural power is doing everything, including dictating each exchange of letters! I think it would be most unreal to not find your many envelopes with "God is Fabulous" stamps waiting when I get home. My heart beats faster just racing to open each letter and read of the marvels of God working constantly daily in your life. Thanks for coming into my life, and I also thank God for including this in his plan.

Time to go to church, so will continue later. Of course, before I can finish yesterday's events, today's fabulous events will also be here to tell you. And it's already swelling up in my whole being that it will really be exciting—see you later today!!

2:00 P.M. About the football game last nite: A few days ago two friends, a couple, called me saying they had four tickets for the Astrodome game Saturday nite and would I like to go? So being completely aware that every invitation to anything for the past two months have directly been events set up by God for a specific purpose, I accepted gladly. Then the lady said they had this odd ticket, but they didn't

51

know how I felt if they invited this lady friend to go, so this was great because again God was setting the scene. I didn't know who she was, but all day Saturday I felt it was going to be something a lot more special than a football game in the Astrodome—and it was! Their guest was Mary, a lady who once was a Christian working in church. She is divorced from her husband (who is now in jail for armed robbery) and is now living in an apartment down the street from my home. She works for one of the airlines and has recently taken several trips trying to find a degree of peace from this.

The game started. University of Houston quickly made a touchdown and the famous $2,000,000 scoreboard flashed on in all its splendor, all 474 feet (length) of it—longer than a football field. Then a few minutes more and another touchdown, and another spectacular. And then God's green light flashed in all its heavenly splendor and I started talking to Mary via the Holy Spirit furnishing all thoughts and words. Mary said when I asked what church she attended, that she had checked several but only one a long way from her apartment gave her any satisfaction; and really her spiritual life had become a vacuum. Then one of either Major Ian Thomas' or your remarks came out and I said, "Great, that is just the way God needs you—in a vacuum spiritually—so he can fill that vacuum the way he wants it." This type of talk with an intertwining of your experiences and mine lasted through the first half and into the half-time show and Mary began to respond to the Holy Spirit showing her the way to really be happy in Christ. Then the evening went along with a very enjoyable air and only occasionally God re-entering the conversation. When I left her about midnight I knew that God had taken her just as far as he needed to but I know we will have another meeting which will bring her back into God's fold, surrendered more completely than ever before, and hopefully to "total surrender." She knows to "turn loose" can give excitement. The Holy Spirit did His consistently perfect job of entering her heart, so now the next step only awaits his nudge and I'm anxious to move!!!

Back to June!! At 4:30 Friday afternoon I stopped by to say hello to her. She was not the same June. Her face was radiant with joy, her voice had excitement in it; when I asked, "How is it going?" She said, "Marvelous!" And she did the witnessing for about 30 minutes! She said two different times this week one of the employers said, "June, what has happened—your whole attitude has changed." Then she told me of a youngish client who had studied for the ministry and then something happened that made him bitter toward God and he is a heavy drinker, etc. She has been talking to him and is letting him read Ian Thomas' *Saving Life of Christ* which she loves (me too!). She said, "Can you imagine, me wandering around in the wilderness seven years when I could have been having milk and honey instead of manna (from Thomas' book)?" She has surrendered her life to Christ—PTL!

She talked about her boss and I do believe God will open up with a double-barrel shot from June and me and grab him for Christ—this of course is to wait until we get the green light. I'm not sure if I told you, but the next day after June and I talked for an hour about ten days ago (boy! think how God changed her life in ten days!) her boss came in and said he had never seen such happiness in anyone as he saw in me and asked June what had happened. She said he has found complete peace with God!

At 5:00 P.M. today I go to June's home for a bar-b-qued chicken dinner, then to church for our next film and discussion and then rush her home to come back to my home where I'll be talking to a young man (17) who gave his heart to Christ when I spoke at the dude ranch in August.

His girl friend left him and he is terribly confused, jealous and disappointed and says he needs to talk with me. When he does, God's Holy Spirit will really give him something stronger than his former beautiful and lovely girl friend to hold onto (and he really was holding her).

I was at a football game Friday nite with the choir director and his wife and again with them Saturday morning. God is really working in their lives. He was explaining to me that I needed to "turn loose" with my voice and let it go because we try to force it into all kinds of binds and it will work far better by itself —how this compares with our lives—if we try to bind them into our way they don't have the freedom God intends.

Oh, yes, that reminds me—last Sunday nite I wrote "turn loose" on a business card and gave it to June. She said Friday she put it in her purse where all week long every time she opened her purse she saw it!! PTL!

That's probably the highlight of the past three

days!!! These letters seem to almost be a diary—I've never written about many of my experiences, except the "thing" I'm writing—whatever it will be. Have you considered taping your public speeches? I have wondered if God wants us to keep tab on such, or does he want to "tell us when we get there" what to say. Have you kept any notes, memos, etc. of the "happenings" God gives you?

"What created the greatest spurt in my Christian growth?" This is a very deep question which was answered to a great extent over a period of a year or more, but which really was answered in about two very simple minutes. Many times in my 40 years of Christian environment (30 years as a Christian) I reached the point of God squarely challenging me to surrender all; each time I said no because I just wouldn't turn loose—mostly, not even knowing what it was I wouldn't turn loose. Then in about May, 1968, at age 47 (almost 48) I knelt at the altar of our church along with perhaps a dozen men at 7:10 A.M. and with no one except God and me knowing, and with no pressure, no sermon, no song challenging me, I, in completely honest and sincere prayer, asked God to take my life and Jeanne's life spiritually, completely and make them what they should be; and, with Jeanne facing surgery which seemed to have little to do with this, I told God to take Jeanne's life physically if necessary, or my life or both or neither, but to, at any *cost,* make us what he wanted us to be.

And how abundantly he did. How marvelously good he has been to me to go beyond anything I could ever imagine to assure me he is a loving God looking after every little need with astounding understanding and so very real and alive. His Spirit living in me totally, miraculously, constantly controls every minute of my life and moves always just like the cloud over the children of Israel—always there for full assurance that he is my God, and that there is no other need in my life except him. Just the overwhelming recalling of his goodness in a complete answer to my prayer floods my soul with such a profound joy that tears flow as freely as the living water he gives which never lets us thirst again because he so completely supplies all we need or desire.

Jeanne completely turned her life over to God in the way I had prayed and was given six months of the greatest, most beautiful, happy life of anyone I have ever known, even through six months of sickness and then into a death approached with a complete faith in God, so perfect that two people, deeply in love with each other and more completely in love with our Lord Jesus Christ and our God, parted with a thrilling, unquestioning happiness I never dreamed could be possible. This really completed the answer to my prayer when I turned loose of my life and gave it all to God. Since that time many great, thrilling miracles and experiences have happened, which have so abundantly assured me that his answer to our release to him of everything only means he may take everything but when he does he gives back a hundred times more than he takes and what he gives back is so much greater than what he takes, but we must turn loose and let him do it His way!

Fran, this in a very condensed way was the heart of what changed my life and let God's Holy Spirit release his power in my life and cause me to just be available and let him do everything and he is changing lives daily through this temple which is all his. Of course, during a period of over a year now, he has read the Word of God to me for hundreds of hours, his way of talking to us; he has supplied exactly the right books at the right time, he has brought into my life (and Jeanne's) several people who have profoundly influenced the way he is preparing me, but all in all it was just surrendering all at any cost and discovering the secret of turning loose and letting God do everything—no effort or decisions or actions left to me except to be available. I could write books of miracles and of experiences and if it would be your desire to expand what I have said, I'll do so, but I hope this may aid in your writing your booklet to help Christians to grow in their Christian life. Some way deeply, which you understand, but within our acquaintance only a few understand, I have the feeling that the real growth that fully counts can only be accomplished with giving all, and then being able to say about anything which confronts us, "It just really doesn't matter to us"— we trust him to do all action in our lives.

How I thrilled talking to you for 45 minutes last nite. I feel so close to you and God and Christ from all these ways of communicating! Please never hesitate to call because it would take too long. I promise that if you only have 5 minutes I'll "hush up" on time. I hesitate to call you because of interrupting you at the most inconvenient time—such as at Spiritual Law #4 or some other place.

Time to go to work. I'd much rather do other

things like writing, but God's field includes a lot of wonderful clients which now beckon me.

In His thrilling love,
Charles

*　　*　　*

November 24, 1969
Miami, Florida
(Letter enclosing manuscript of *Hot Line to Heaven*)

Charles, dear:

Before you read this, ask God's Holy Spirit to reveal to you any weaknesses or needs in the book, will you?

And pray for the response and the effect of the book.

Because I believe in prayer,
Frances

*　　*　　*

Houston, Texas
Monday, November 24, 1969

Dear Fran,

This one must be short after the 12 pages I mailed this morning!

This, of course, has been another fabulous day, to wit:

1. June: Last nite she said a man at their office just didn't rub her right and irritated her—so we talked of loving your enemies. I suggested that she read the 13th chapter of 1st Corinthians every morning and every time she feels bugged by him to say to herself, "I love you" and if she felt like it to say it aloud to him. About 10:00 this A.M. she phoned to

say that when he came by her desk she smiled and in a very friendly manner said, "Good morning," and he, surprised, came back in a little while to talk. He needed two new employees and by noon God had supplied both for him. June knows what we mean by turning loose—full surrender and she has had three or four things happen already to see how God acts when we ask and expect him to do what he wants—not what we plan.

I think it was Saturday that she had Ian Thomas' book *Saving Life of Christ.* She passed by a friend's apartment, below hers. The door was open and a policeman was inside, so June inquired to find that her friend's TV console had been stolen. Her friend was completely lost. "What am I going to do without a TV?" June said, "Read this book," and so she recognized another of God's convenient ways.

Today her boss and another executive became friendly for the first time in a year. Quite eventful for someone new to complete surrender. PTL. She is joining our choir tomorrow nite.

2. You may recall the lady accountant we hired about 2 weeks ago because God said "no" to one we selected and then right after noon Dixie came in. She's a fine Christian and a most excellent accountant. I feel very close to her and get excited telling her of the fantastic events. Today she told me what God really did to send her to us. Her husband had come home for no particular reason about 10:00 that morning; and out of a clear blue sky mentioned to her that he thought she was going to go to work. She said probably after Thanksgiving—then the phone rang. Her friend, an employment agent, also a

friend of our secretary, was calling Dixie, and said she had a good, prospective job (Dixie hadn't even applied) and for her to come down right away, although she thought the position was filled. Dixie said she wasn't dressed. The agent said, "Put on anything, but hurry." Dixie did and was in our office after noon talking about the job and God, and went home to tell her husband she had a job. She is quite excited about being a part of a fabulous day because I told her within 30 minutes after she arrived that God had sent her.

What am I going to tell you new when I get to Miami? I'll just bask in your spiritual sunshine and listen!!

Just made reservations and might change the return trip.

12-23 Tues.—Leave Houston 7:00 A.M. Flt. 28. National Airlines to Tampa, Florida; arrive 10:32 A.M. My brother and his wife will meet me and drive to Miami—with me exciting them for 5 hours about a "Living" God and what turning loose really means.

12-23 Tues. Nite—Will call you when I get there— Fabulous!

12-23 to New Year's. I'm yours as much as you can put up with me but I'll get out of your way and be with them. Don't know where I'll stay, but will find out from them soon and let you know. Please don't plan to disrupt your plans for such a long stay, but just let me know times you do have me included and you have No. 1AAA priority!

My brother, his wife and I will leave Miami on New Year's Day or the 2nd and go to Bessemer. He wants me to speak in Sunday's service—now isn't that something—I've never done anything like that but if God lets these plans all go through HE will do the talking! I didn't plan to stay so long, but I felt God nudge and say do it while talking to Clyde tonite, so!! I'll have plenty of new excitement after visiting you—WOW!! This is going to be the greatest New Year's ever and I've got a feeling 1970 will be a whole year of the greatest in both our lives!

I'm really anxious to get *Hot Line to Heaven* and drink in every thrilling word and cry right along with you as the Holy Spirit talks of His power when he has such an invitation to run a life fully given to him. It's really sad that God tries to get Christians to understand this is for all and so few trust him enough to accept his phenomenal gifts. Hurry with your manuscript!! This is a great privilege to be close enough to you to be invited to read it and I'm really longing for it. I already know it's tremendous!

I'm leaving Houston early Thursday morning to go to Corpus Christi to spend Thanksgiving with my parents and Friday afternoon to a lake 50 miles from Corpus to see my oldest brother Milton and his wife Mary and will return Saturday by 6 or 7 P.M. Hope your manuscript arrives before I leave.

I've been writing an hour and 7 pages—a short letter! But I sorta like visiting you and this is second best to talking to you—next best is a letter from you.

With God's richest blessings on your new book and you, I bid you

Goodnite,
Charles

*   *   *

Monday, November 24, 1969
Miami, Florida

Dearest Charles:

Just a real quick note to let you know I'm probably the baggiest-eyed gal in Miami today. I was so completely wound up after sharing with you last night that I simply couldn't go to sleep. Peculiarly, because of all the personal things I hear while I'm on tour, I've learned never to open my mouth and never to share my personal thoughts with anyone, and all of a sudden I've discovered a desire to share each and every excitement with you.

I went to an absolutely FABULOUS breakfast this morning (even if I was baggy-eyed). Several businessmen asked me to come to a breakfast this morning to discuss the possibility of having a "soul-saving station" at the County Youth Fair which will be held here in January. You know . . . one of those "step right up, have the four Spiritual Laws read to you, absolutely FREE!" I've never been involved completely in one of these things, but I think it could be an absolutely fabulous thing, don't you? So if you hear that I've turned out to be a barker in a circus, you'll know why. "I'm a fool for Christ's sake—whose fool are you?" Don't tell me, because I know —you're a fool for Christ's sake, too! And that's scriptural, because that's what Paul said.

Tonight I'm going to dinner with Pat Boone! How 'bout that? Well, not really, but they're having the initial banquet concerning a Miami Christian TV station, and I've been invited. I think it's going to be a fabulous thing. I heard about this a couple of years ago. I'm going with the president of the Fellowship of Churches, Pappy Howland and his wife; Ted Place, executive director of Youth for Christ and a couple of others. I'm taking a woman along who needs to have a deeper commitment to Christ. It's peculiar—seems like all your spiritual enrichment work is with women—and I really shy away from the men because so many times I discover they think they're going to fall in love with me so I have to turn them over to the pastor or to other men. I'm sure you are discovering the same thing. When you are of spiritual assistance to someone, they temporarily look upon you as Jesus Christ and then comes the battle of making them keep their eyes on Christ.

I may have told you when I first became a Christian, I honestly thought my pastor was Jesus Christ, and he had a time convincing me that he wasn't, because every time I'd thank him for something, he'd say, "Don't thank me, thank the Lord!" But it's funny how this experience has been so invaluable in my own life because my request to each church has always been that when I leave they would not remember me (or Frances Gardner as I put it) but would only remember that God's Holy Spirit had moved in their life and I pray that they only see Christ and nothing else. As a matter of fact, Gulf Coast was a good example of this, because at the last service there I made them sing "Let Me See Jesus Only." The kids especially have a tendency to put a human on a pedestal, but this does *nothing* for their Christian life, and that was why I felt it so very essential to remind them to keep their eyes on Christ. I remember the story of Peter who did so well walking

63

on the water, until he took his eyes off of Christ, and then glub, glub, glub, down he went.

I'm not going to write you any more, because I don't want to take any more time of yours—I want you to use it reading my newest book. I'm sure I don't have to tell you to be careful to see it is not read by others because of the copyright infringement, but somehow or other, I wanted to share it with you.

Charles, this will probably be the last letter you get before Thanksgiving, unless the mail is exceptionally fast, but I do want you to know that in my Thanksgiving prayers there is a very special one thanking God for changing my mind concerning the first thing I ever said about you. You must remember I knew nothing about you, and you may also have noticed the ice in my voice when I talked to you on the telephone, and when I hung up, I said to the girl who was also working, "That *dirty old man*—he asked me if I wanted to stay at his house!" . . . then I went on to say, "What does he think I am, and who does he think he is!" . . . and you will remember I asked you to contact the college president because he was making all the arrangements, and yet I wonder what made me turn the page of my schedule when I got it, to look first of all to see if your name was on there—and it was! There are so many things I have to be thankful for this year—and knowing you is right at the top of the list.

Because He loves, I love,

Frances

(Handwritten note)

Charles—May this be your most blessed Thanksgiving and may God pour out upon you even greater blessings in this coming year.

P.S. I'm going to let you teach my Sunday School class while you're here. More on the holiday season in my next letter. . . . Continuation. . . . Don't you wish I'd shut up?

Please remember to pray for God's traveling mercies as we drive on Thanksgiving Day to Clearwater for the Youth Convention, and then pray that God will make me a blessing to all the youth who will be attending my conferences on witnessing.

We're having a pitch-in dinner and special service Thanksgiving Eve. These we always do by candlelight and they're fabulous.

No more . . . no more . . . no more until later.

If I don't stop—this will never get mailed. Just remembered something else. I had called my publisher last night to tell them the last chapter was en route and they told me that *Go, Man, Go* had its third printing last week, and it's only seven months old.

Frances

*   *   *

Miami, Florida, November 25, 1969

Dearest Charles:

Joan brought a typewriter home from the office to do some school typing, and it's still here, so thought I'd type you a few lines before I go to work today.

Isn't it awful to feel like I did last night that I just *had to share with you* the excitement of Pat and

Shirley Boone? I have never seen a couple where the love of Christ shone through both of them in their personal love affair. It was so completely thrilling to me I just melted, and if you don't think I was having a time with my old contact floating—whenever I get emotional like that, it fogs my contact and sure makes seeing hard. The woman sitting next to me said, "If they'd said one more sentence, I would have cried." I said, "They didn't stop soon enough for me not to cry. P.T.L." It was just gorgeous. Probably the reason it affected me so much was it made me think of the life of Tom and Jan. Last night when I left them at the office to run home and get dressed, Brant (my grandson) was charging around the parking lot in his walker (he is really a doll—but I could be prejudiced) and Tom and Jan were standing there and I looked at these two good-looking young people (Jan is 5'1"—tiny and blonde and *beautiful;* Tom is 6'3"—brown-eyed and dark and considered very handsome) and just speculated on what could happen to their marriage when Christ takes first place. And then I looked at them as they really are— without Christ and so completely lost it's pathetic. I just said, "When, Lord, when . . . ?"

Pat Boone has just finished making a movie of *The Cross and the Switchblade* where he portrays Dave Wilkerson. I haven't seen a movie in three years, but that's going to be on my list somehow, somewhere. He told of standing on a corner in Harlem preaching (as Dave Wilkerson) and then they asked him to come back and preach as Pat Boone, so he went back, and said, "If anyone had ever told me a year ago that I'd be standing on a street corner preaching,

I would never have believed it, and then he told me how he and Shirley have found the real JOY through total surrender. He said they're not concerned about their future, or about his job, or anything else, because they're safe and secure in God's plan . . . it was so typical of what you write and how I feel and so un"typical" of the majority of Christians. Talk about a couple who "hang loose with Jesus." I couldn't help but feel what a boon (and what a pun that is) they are to the married couples of today who are missing something in their marriage.

I don't know if I mentioned to you that I had taken both of my books along to give them and when I did, Pat said, "Oh, we've got *Go, Man, Go!*" I promised them a copy of *Hot Line* when it comes off the press. By the way, if you'll look at the inside cover of the *Book Store Journal* you will see an ad for his new album "Rapture" which contains all songs about the second coming of Christ. He said, "If that ceiling opened right now and we all went straight up, it would be all right with me!"

I looked at my telephone last night after I hung up and it brought to my mind the part in my book about the direct line to God that we all have, and I was probably more impressed with this last night than I ever had been, because I have one of those small phones with the buttons in the receiver (do you have those in Houston yet?) and all I did was to push 1-713-000-0000 and there you were. Are you aware of the fact that it's more trouble and work to call you up than it is to call up God? Never quite thought about it that way before.

Joan really enjoyed last night. I know you'll enjoy

meeting Joan—she's my butterball, but losing weight (P.T.L.) and she has a far greater spiritual depth than most 16-year-olds (and don't faint when you meet her—she's taller than I am) and this spiritual depth is fabulous, but it makes it difficult for her with other kids her own age, because they just can't understand. I've told her not to worry, because in the final analysis she'll see who comes out on top, but she loves to go to things like last night. She really enjoys being around the college kids in Campus Crusade for Christ, because they live and breathe the same Christ that she does. She was really floating on a cloud when we came home.

Can't wait for the mailman to bring your letters. I used to watch the mail for the checks coming into the office and then finally got around to opening the rest of the stuff, but now I throw the checks to one side and look for that Houston postmark. And that reminds me, you'd better be careful, because I've saved all your letters and might print a book called "Letters from Charles." Your letters are so beautiful, Charles, because I see the Christ in you in everything you write and I can almost actually feel the love of God which flows from every word. And I know how long it takes to write letters in longhand, and how tedious it is, and that's why I probably doubly appreciate them because I know what you have to give up to write to me.

I'm really praying that the Lord will show me all the people He wants you to meet in Miami. I want your holiday season to be absolutely perfect, so I don't want to mess it up with individuals who just don't hang in there with God, but then I also wonder if a few of them might not be good, too, because I still believe there is more Christianity caught than was ever taught—and yet in your case, from what little I know it would seem to me the great closeness you have with God was caused by all the reading that you did during Jeanne's illness.

I was so delighted to know that you're going to spend Thanksgiving with your folks. I'm sure they'll enjoy having you with them, and you may feel free to read them whatever parts of the book you want to. I forgot to ask you, are they Christians? That's probably a dumb question to ask, but I never take anything for granted. Well, Christian or not, I'll be praying that your visit with them will enlarge their idea of what Christ can do in a totally surrendered life. I couldn't help but think that this year brought great sorrow into your life but from the sorrow arose the greatest victory in your life—and it reminded me of the tragedy of losing the sight of one of my eyes was the thing that brought me the greatest victory. Did you ever notice that people who have actually reached the heights have been sent there through tragedy? Not always, but in many, many instances this is the case, and then this person is the type who really seeks more and more and more of God.

I was reading from the *Living Letters* this morning —Colossians 3:10 and 11. "You are living a brand new kind of life that is ever learning MORE AND MORE of what is right, and trying to be MORE AND MORE like Christ Who created this new life within you. In this new life one's nationality or race or education or social position is unimportant. Such things mean nothing; whether a person has Christ is what matters, and He is equally available to all." I love that part "whether a person has Christ is what matters." And that's all that really matters, isn't it? Because then we know that we can relax and have absolutely no concern for the future knowing that He is leading us the right way. Then I read the Love Chapter in I Corinthians, which in the Revised Standard is one of the most beautiful of all the passages. I guess it's because I cut my spiritual teeth on the Revised Standard that I particularly like that version and especially the 13th chapter.

Again, my thoughts will be with you on Thanksgiving Day and my prayers will be joining with yours because there are times when I'm praying and somehow or other, I know your prayers are joining mine on the way up to God.

May God grant you traveling mercies as you go to Corpus Christi, may He make you a blessing to all you meet while you're there, and then may He bring you safely back to Houston and may He, through all of this, enrich your life to a greater degree than you ever dreamed possible.

In His abiding love,

Frances

* * *

Special Note:
November 25, 1969
Miami, Florida

I thought the Bible said: "Follow me, and I will make you fishers of men." I think you misunderstood this to read: "Follow me, and I will make you a *hunter* of women." (BIG PUN—) How 'bout that for a new translation.

*   *   *

AUTHOR'S NOTE: I never cease to be amazed at how God works or at the way he communicates His plan for our life. But after talking to Charles on the telephone the night of November 25th, I retired for the night when all of a sudden at 1:30 in the morning of the 26th I was utterly compelled to jump out of bed and run for my Bible. I do not know how God communicates, but I do know this . . . God told me to get out of bed and go to the Old Testament because He had some scripture I was to memorize. Some people feel it's an instantaneous thought, but whatever it is, it doesn't take anything except "instant" obedience to someone walking in the spirit, because there is a definite awareness of God's presence and His will.

My bedroom was completely enveloped with the presence of God and I immediately got out of bed and ran for my favorite Bible (RSV) but to my dismay I discovered that I had left it at my office. I said, "God, do you want me to put my clothes on and go back to the office and get my favorite Bible at this hour of the morning, or would it read the same in the King James?" It seemed clear to me that I should get the King James. Now here's an interesting thing . . . I ALWAYS carry my Revised Standard with me. It goes with me when I go out the door to go to the store, it goes with me when I have any kind of an appointment . . . it goes with me on every airplane trip . . . it's just as much a part of me as anything I have or own, but peculiarly, this night God had allowed me to leave it in my office. Now I know why—then I didn't. I ran for my King James and KNEW God's message was in the Old Testament, so I began to thumb through the pages not knowing what I was looking for because I had not been a student of the Old Testament before this, but I was tingling with excitement because I knew this was something very special. It didn't take me long to discover what God had for me this night! . . . because when God has something for you, he quickly lets you know exactly what it is.

Two verses of scripture jumped out at me, and as I read them, cold chills ran up and down my spine, because GOD HAD TOLD ME TO MEMORIZE THE TWO VERSES OF SCRIPTURE WHICH WOULD BE MY ANSWER TO CHARLES WHEN HE ASKED ME TO MARRY HIM, AND NEVER IN A LETTER OR ON A PHONE CALL HAD THE THOUGHT OF LOVE OR MAR-RIAGE EVER ENTERED THE CONVERSA-TION. Both of our lives are so Christ centered it seemed there wasn't time for anything else, and yet here I sat completely electrified by God's presence and instantly memorized the two verses He had given to me. It's a very interesting fact that I have never been able to memorize a tremendous amount of scripture. I suppose when you're not real young any more, the mind just doesn't memorize quite so fast (although let me assure you I get the message) but this night God allowed me to memorize the verses in just a few short seconds as they were indelibly burned into my mind. I only said, "I don't know how you're going to do it, Lord, but I've done what you've told me to do!" Then I went to my desk, sat down at the typewriter, and typed the following on one of my business cards to Charles:

Nov. 26, 1969, 2 A.M.—I was utterly *compelled* to search out a verse of scripture and memorize it (actually two). In God's perfect timing, I'll tell you the verses. In the meantime, please hold this in your wallet.

Frances

Then I wrote the following letter, signed it, put the card and letter in an envelope and addressed it to Charles.

*　　*　　*

Miami, Florida
November 26, 1969

Dearest Charles:

This one isn't a letter, but just a request that you put this in your wallet.

After reading your letter this morning, this really gave me the chills.

In His magnificence,
Frances

Note: After this, I went to bed and slept with the angels, having been obedient to God.

*　　*　　*

Miami, Florida, November 26, 1969

Dearest Charles:

Switched typewriters on you, didn't I? But decided I could get more on the page with this one. Just simply HAD to write to you again to keep you abreast of the times. Richard, my beloved spiritual child, came home this morning about 3:15. I had locked the doors, so he rapped on Joan's window and she got up and let him in, and I didn't even hear him come in. He had called and asked me to put a sheet on the living room sofa for him to sleep, so I did, and when I woke up this morning I thought, "What happened to Richard?" I said a real fast little prayer for his safety, went tearing out into the living room and there he was. He's always such a joy, and he'll be home at Christmastime and he's real anxious to meet you.

And you can tell from the back of the other envelope that I shared a portion of your letter with Joan (and also with Richard) and she very slyly asked me a while ago if I had looked at the letter to you in my purse and I said, "No, did you read it?" And she smugly said, "No—but you should see what I did to it." I went and looked and she really wanted you to see *God Is Fabulous* when you get home from work, didn't she? She's really anticipating meeting you and sharing the excitement of Christ which I keep telling her about concerning you.

Your letter thrilled me beyond words—just about everything. I don't know when anyone ever communicated so beautifully their total surrender as you did in your letter. And your love of Jeanne was beautifully and eloquently expressed so that it was all I could do to keep from crying as I read not your words, but your very soul pouring out its innermost thoughts.

Charles, you have an absolutely beautiful way of communicating your thoughts, and I'm going to pray that sometime I'll be able to talk you into writing a book. (Or maybe I'll just pray and ask our God to communicate this thought to you.) I'm so thrilled to see how God is using you in the lives of so many individuals—even at football games (did you ever watch the game?). And June's progress sounds unreal it's so fast.

Somehow I didn't seem to take off so fast, I'll be real honest with you, it seems to me I had to do everything the hard way and fight with God at every turn, but never once did my original desire change—but I kept wanting to do it my way, and God really had to hit me on the head several times and still does, I guess, although not nearly as much as formerly. I just reread the little part in your letter about turning your voice loose—and it struck me real funny because of what I had just said and you said, "if we try to bind them into *our way* they don't have the freedom God intends." So true, so true, because it's only when we *believe the whole truth* that the truth sets us completely free.

And don't tell anybody, but now I know how old you are (you infant) and I thought your comment was excellent where you told your age when you said, "with no pressure, no sermon, no song challenging me" you squarely and honestly asked God to take all of you.

WEEEEEELLLLLLLL . . . between the last sentence and now Joan came back to the office after taking Richard down to his folks to stay for the night, and then I got to talk to you. All I can say is a great big P.T.L. I wonder if you don't think it might be a good idea if we bought a telephone company—I hate to think of the telephone bills for just this week. But I could have really talked all night to you without ever running out of conversation—but then God never runs out of miracles, does he? And just as your letter said—our lives have been so completely apart for so long, and if memory serves me correctly, I met you on Friday, October 3rd, at approximately 7:15 P.M. a little less than 2 months ago, saw you on Saturday morning briefly at the breakfast, saw you Sunday afternoon when you took me to your church and back, and then after the service and at Bill and Suzanne Menefee's house. Do you realize what a few hours we've ever actually seen each other, and yet so much has been communicated in your letters I find it hard to believe it was such a short time. And if you want to think of something really hilarious, are you aware that much of that time was spent in my talking to a church. I want you to think how very, very little of that time was spent in just talking to each other. Oh, well, we really talk to God anyway and maybe that's why there seems to be no barrier concerning the short length of time we've known each other.

. . . and then just to whet your appetite, someday I'll tell you what Max Gaulke said to me as he told me goodbye at the airport. And in case you're interested, when the big jet took off and I looked down at Houston I closed my eyes briefly and said, "Lord, you didn't throw me a curve, did you?" And I'll let you guess what I was thinking about. (Or who.)

I'm glad you said when you talked to me tonight that you liked HLTH *(Hot Line to Heaven)*. But please ask God to reveal to you any of the weaknesses which are in it. I'm always so emotionally exhausted and drained when a book is completed, that it's hard for me to go back and read it with any degree of intelligence. Somehow or other I always feel (when I finish a book) like Jesus did when the woman touched the hem of his garment: The power went from me. It seems the reservoir is empty for just a brief while, and then God's Holy Spirit fills it up again—normally the urge for another book doesn't come this soon again, but I'm bubbling over with *Hang Loose with Jesus*.

Please remember to pray for Joanie that God's healing touch and his great Holy Spirit will breathe upon her during her stay in the hospital. I'm scheduled to be away next weekend and I really wanted to cancel it, but Joan insists she's going to be all right, so I'm going anyway, because that isn't very far. I have several daytime churches where I'll be speaking next week and then I have a speaking engagement Wednesday Dec. 10th in the evening in Miami, and also on Friday, Dec. 12th in Lake Worth which I'll drive to and back Friday evening. Apparently from the schedule they've changed my time in Alabama so I won't be going up until Monday. I was really wondering because that would have been a tremendous amount of commuting for me to be in Huntsville and then back to Birmingham for TV and it seems about four trips in between. This gives me an extra weekend in my own church which will also be good.

And thanks for giving me first chance at your time in Miami. Since I have the first choice, I'll just be very *unselfish* and take *all* of it. After all, I just don't want you to worry about what to do with yourself while you're down here, so I'll *suffer* through every minute with you. In the meantime, I'm going to be cramming on my Bible reading—you're far more knowledgeable on the Bible than I am, so I'll just have to do some real cramming.

Can't tell you what a thrill it was (but then I don't have to, do I?) to hear from you again tonight. My prayers and thoughts will be winging their way to Corpus Christi tomorrow and I'll be praying for God's traveling mercies for both of us on a most thrilling and blessed Thanksgiving Day. And I'm so thankful that I'll be sharing with you in person in less than a month.

Because He lives in your heart and mine,

Frances

*   *   *

AUTHOR'S NOTE: The following letter from Charles was one of the funniest I ever received, although it didn't exactly strike me that way at the time I read it, but note as God was drawing the holy circle of matrimony close around us, he used a member of each of our families to plant the idea of marriage into our minds. As you read the following letter, please remember that no thought had ever crossed Charles' mind about the possibility of our getting married, but watch how he fumbled through the thoughts he had.

In the process of writing this book, I reread part of this letter to Charles and with the honest approach he always has to everything, he said, "I guess that's when I really proposed, isn't it?" Then he added, "But I sure did it the hard way!"

Houston, Texas
November 26, 1969

Dearest Fran,

Tonite (as always) *Hot Line to Heaven* is answering better than 1-305-000-0000. Sure hope you didn't decide to go to Clearwater tonite instead of tomorrow; don't think I can stand waiting all through the holidays to talk to you.

WOW! *Hot Line to Heaven* IS GREAT!!!!

It's exciting, thrilling, searching, deep, joyful, fabulous, and really it's again God telling of his magnificent love through a wonderful lady who is absolutely nothing but who is utterly everything because the Holy Spirit dwells constantly in her surrendered life.

Then a marvelous conversation with the most exciting person except Christ I know—it's great to know you both! After my call last nite, I didn't try to do more writing. The day had ended so perfectly!

Thanksgiving—8:30 P.M.—Corpus Christi

I'm glad you had such a great day today going to Clearwater and being involved with Christ changing the lives of the youth and probably a lot of "oldths" also! I'll be anxious for a fill-in of details. I already know it was great!

It took four and a half hours to come to my parents home and would you believe they were fabulous?! Sure you would! The first half was spent in just talking to God and even shedding a few tears as He talked with me, and sometimes I felt you were in the middle of the conversation because you are most always in the middle of my thoughts. Thoughts of God and thoughts of you are so very much alike because you belong to Him. I wrote several mental paragraphs to you while driving so I hope some of them get on paper tonite.

One thing I have for quite some time been planning to do is to have some more appropriate stationery printed so my thoughts went something like this:

I would want a designed stationery that had life in it, something that would communicate with whoever saw it the one central theme of my life—TURN LOOSE; would find a way to have love slip into the subconscious mind of the viewer or reader. It might even have a semihidden watermark like "God is Fabulous—Turn Loose." In some way it would have a silk-screen spray of the Holy Spirit blended into its color, and then be treated, just before it is printed, with a prayer from Frances so that it and the words to be written on it would really cause people of all walks of life to know that only by full and complete surrender can anything really exciting ever happen in their lives. Only one person I know is close enough to God to ask him to use her experience and imagination and his direction to create something like this, but it could really be something special. Now, I don't mean I'm asking you to do a design job, because you know you are out of the printing business, but I do ask that you ask God to let us know a way to really communicate with others—if he considers that part of what I'm to do. I think your stationery really sends a message in the same way your writing, talking and praying does.

I have had a great visit with my Mother; and Papa is alert enough today that he listened for over an hour to his excited son tell of fantastic events God is arranging and using me to carry out. I get so thrilled telling about what God does, that I'm already telling another story before I finished the last two. You have my Mother dreaming about you, and I don't really recall mentioning you during the past three or four weeks, because she is hard of hearing and I don't get into many particulars by phone with her. (I phone her once a week instead of writing.) Now, I could just not tell her dream and let you be curious, but that wouldn't be very nice so here is what she dreamed about two weeks ago.

I (Charles) was talking with Frances Gardner and telling her that God didn't care whether we were working in a church in Houston or a church in Miami because God can use born again Christians any-where. She has read *God Is Fabulous* (before I met you) and she sees the most excited son in her family and probably in her life, and probably your excite-ment related to my excitement resulted in her dream of us talking with each other. Then what she said sorta stunned me, and I probably shouldn't relate it to you, but I seem to tell you everything: I had told her how for the past month we had been exchanging letters and phone calls and that I, as well as my brother and his wife would be in Miami Christmas and suddenly, "Are you going to get married?" It took a bit of explaining that we both were fully and totally serving God, that we had no idea even why we were brought together in the ways we have been and that whatever our future was, we really didn't care and that only God would do any planning.

Now until we talked, I guess last night, no

thoughts had particularly even come up about why we are together and as we discussed (or maybe I said) I have not really felt that God would so completely use us as he did with Paul if either of us ever married anyone. Maybe I should destroy this page and talk about something I know about, because I really have no idea what he has in mind for my life and my only determined desire is for him to continue day by day to make every decision for me and let me know what I am to do. For certain, I did not have any motive or thought related to my New Year's Eve Party-for-the-Lord trip to Miami than to be there for a terrific party just to be in the joy of God's service with the thrill of being a part of God's plan for my life.

In case this doesn't read to you like it does to me, I'm concerned that I might "turn you off" as a marvelous friend which I prize so dearly, by either mentioning the word marriage like I was interested or like I was not interested. Only last nite in our talk and this question by Mama do I even recall any discussion that could relate to this being of any significance. And really, this has been no part of my feeling. I've been so busy being thrilled with our exchange of letters, calls and plans for Miami and plans to be with you, and so completely elated at the wonder of what God's plans for us spiritually really are, but knowing something specific and great is in his plans, that no thoughts otherwise really emerged. I know God has for 1970 for both of us some fantastic programs and truly I believe with all my heart he will tell us when we need to know why this sudden, close, wonderful friendship has developed. I love it! And I'm thrilled to know whatever he makes of our being together will be just right for both of us and that we have no concern about his answer. It will be good regardless of the way he answers. Please, if you have any feeling that might bother you about what I have so inadequately and poorly muddled above, tell me. How did I get into this discussion? And should I have? PTL Someway!

TOTALLY NEW SUBJECT. I don't know what it will be! I'm anxious to go back through *Hot Line to Heaven* again. I really believe it will top the other two books or at least equal them. When I say equal them, how can you top the top?! I feel so very highly honored to have the manuscript to read and live, with you right near by means of telephone, letters and something indescribably near to me. There is just no way I can find to tell you how I feel about all of our "together" ways. I know spending the holidays with you will be wonderful; I'm getting anxious!!

How did you like not having a bologna sandwich this Thanksgiving—or did you, just for old times sake?!

My prayers follow you wherever you are and I know God honors them as a little boost to the prayers you pray for the effective mission of your speaking. I'll add special prayers for *Hang Loose with Jesus.* Your goodnite prayers by phone mean a lot—and you mean a lot to me.

Goodnite in a special way,
Charles

*   *   *

AUTHOR'S NOTE: God is SO fabulous! Thanksgiving time is always a very special time in the life of almost everyone as we take time out to think about our special blessings and the things we have to be thankful for. Even most non-Christians do observe Thanksgiving as a time of remembering (for a little while at least) the good things of life. Mine have always been doubly exciting since I became a Christian, because I have spent each Thanksgiving at a Youth Convention in the State of Florida, and this year in between seminars I was scribbling the following letter to Charles when all of a sudden my daughter came into my room and with absolutely nothing prefacing her statement, she said: "Mother, I wish you'd marry this Charles Hunter." I said, "Joan, get that right out of your mind this instant. You KNOW I'm going to have a mad, wild love affair with God the rest of my life, and I don't have time to think about love or marriage or romance or anything like that! And anyway, it would be impossible because of the call that God has put on my life. There isn't any possible way I could ever think of marrying and yet still run around the country doing what God has called me to do." She just shrugged her shoulders and turned and left the room again saying, "Well, I still think it would be 'cool' if you married him."

With that I dismissed this thought from my mind, so I thought, but note that God used a member of my family to plant the idea of marrying Charles into my mind, just as He had used a member of Charles' family with him.

Joan had had a slight opportunity to become acquainted with Charles, because every night when I

*was scheduled to be at home, we would patiently
wait for the telephone to ring, and when it did, Joan
and I would both madly race to answer it, but since
she's younger than I am, she usually beat me, and
anyway the phone in her room was closer than the
phone in my room, and she'd have some exciting little conversations with Charles, and when she would
finally relinquish the telephone to me, she'd stand at
the foot of my bed and say, as only a 16-year-old
can say when they imitate someone else, "Hel-llllllllo,
Charrrrrrrrrr-llllllllllllllles, Yessssssssssss, Charrrrrrrr-
llllllles, mmmmmmmmmmmmmmm, mmmmmmm-
mmmmm, mmmmmmmmmm," and then as she made
faces at me from the foot of the bed (I had to flop
across my bed to reach the telephone) she'd say,
"Moth------er, you're SOOOOOOOOO silly!" And
then afterwards or the next day I'd have to listen
to a lecture about how ridiculous I behaved (a re-
versal from the norm of a mother telling a teen-age
daughter how silly she's behaving). I'm so glad that
God doesn't reserve love for the young.*

*I'm glad he saves some of it for us older folks, be-
cause we can really appreciate it, but somehow or
other, falling in love at 53 is just the same as it is at
16 (only better). My silly old heart just ran away
every time the telephone rang and every time I
opened a letter from Houston, my heart just wouldn't
be controlled. And it's a funny thing how every single
thought I had concerned God, Christ and Charles.
Somehow or other, there was a great turbulence, because I didn't know what was going to happen in this
situation, but there was also a great peace, because I
knew the entire situation was in God's hands and I*

knew that whatever happened would be for the best.

* * *

Miami, Florida, Thanksgiving night, 1969
(11/27/69)

Dear Charles:

Well, here's another of those handwritten letters, but P.T.L.A. I was so wound up after talking to you last night! It's so unbelievably unreal how God lets us share for an hour, and I could have gone on for hours more—but then I thought about the size of the bill!! But it's fabulous how Christ bridges the gap because under any other circumstances we would be *utter strangers,* but with Christ the common denominator it seems there are no barriers in communicating. P.T.L.

You were so in my thoughts as I drove up here today—it took us about five hours because it was a most "unusual" day for Florida—raining, drizzly, foggy—and not too good for driving, but it couldn't dampen my spirits because I was thinking of our phone conversation and how excited I am about the holidays. I think it's fabulous how God has made it possible for you to be here, but all of a sudden I wondered where I had gotten the courage to ask you to come. Well, a big P.T.L. for whatever gave me the courage.

I'm so thrilled at what you said on the phone about Tom. He has a great desire to be successful, has great talent too, and is impressed with successful men. I pray that you will be the one the Lord uses. When I think what their marriage could be if it were only Christ-centered! But did you ever look at a lot of the marriages of people you know? A lot of them could really use Christ! And I think of your life and mine—so uncomplicated and not fouled up with the nonessentials that bog down most relationships!

When I finally got around to simmering down last night I ran one of the presses so that the church news would go out . . . and I did the unforgivable thing—I got a piece of paper caught in the rollers and I had to clean the whole press. WOW—if that wouldn't try your Christianity! I kept singing "I Am A Child of God" as I got covered with ink! My fingernails are still black tonight—but anyway, at 4:00 A.M. I finally got finished, went home and slept two hours and had to get up at 6:00 to come to Clearwater.

We had our first service of the Youth Convention tonight. Tomorrow I have two conferences—both witnessing which I'm really looking forward to. I really had hysterics when we finally got here because I know so many of the Florida kids, having spoken at rallies, etc. They almost literally tear me apart. Many of them are young people who accepted Christ when I was in their church so naturally I have a real love for them and a real concern to see them grow in Christ! And it really thrilled me to see so many of the new Christians come to the convention.

The entertainer we brought had to do an "Abe Lincoln" thing at a church in Miami this morning, so we attended the service, too. The offering was over $4,000.00 so you know it was a big church. I nearly croaked when the pastor recognized me and asked me to offer the Thanksgiving prayer. He had been in a church in upstate Florida where I spoke. It always fractures me when someone recognizes me because I'm still a real nobody.

I'm really the most ordinary person in the world. I make that statement because I'm glad you'll see me "just as I am," and without the glamour of being the speaker in a church.

There's a real sharp couple from Orlando coming down for New Year's Eve and the next day. I invited them to a small dinner at my "minipartment" and told them I was having a *special* guest from Houston I wanted them to meet. They really need some "going on" help. They're not sharing their faith enough, so I thought you would be duck soup for . . . .

Slight interruption—some of the girls came in for a goodnight kiss. Some of these kids are real dolls.

I had better say goodnight my dear. Hope you can read my thoughts and prayers even if you can't read my writing. I look at your beautiful writing and just about decided to bring a typewriter or not write . . . .

Happy Thanksgiving. By the time you receive this you'll be back home again. I pray the trip to Corpus Christi brought you some real excitement at being with your parents. May God continue to bless you and continue to make you a blessing!

In His great and mighty love!

Frances

* * *

Clearwater, Florida, November 28, 1969

Dearest Charles:

Whoops, where did I get the red pen? Oh, well!

The Youth Convention has really been dragging, so I really prayed the Lord would allow some Holy Spirit work to be done. Well, to make a long story short, I asked how many kids would like to go sidewalk evangelizing with me. At least 100 responded, so we piled them in cars and off we went! Anyway, it was pouring rain and we had asked God for sunshine, it was still raining and we had previously asked for a shopping center with a covered mall, but they told us there wasn't any. Then all of a sudden someone told us where there was one. I went to the manager's office but he was out. When I explained to the secretary, who proved to be a born again Christian, what we wanted to do, she gave us permission, so we brought all the kids in to the center of this huge shopping center. They sat around on the edge of the fountain, sang beautiful Christian Christmas songs. And, of course, the rest of the kids were going to play "follow the leader," so I really prayed for a heart—and *really* prayed for holy boldness and away I went. The Lord really did it so neat—the first gal prayed right there with *all the kids watching.* God has *never* let me down when I claimed the victory for His glory. You couldn't hold the kids after that. They took the survey sheets and really did a job for the Lord!

One station wagon went to the wrong shopping center and ran into a bunch of pseudohippies. They invited them to the service tonight. They had asked us to pray for them. At the banquet tonight I was talking to Leroy Fulton, president of the college, when two of the girls came up and asked me to come with them to get these fifteen kids to the service. Instead of leaving right then, I said, "Let's pray them in." So we prayed that God's Holy Spirit would bring them—and then we called for the convicting power of His Holy Spirit! And claimed their souls!

And would you believe six were saved tonight? Beads, serapes, sandals and all. What a service.

Then they asked me to pray for a young man with multiple sclerosis! It was fabulous. He raised his arms above his head.

The young man we took with us has been very interesting—you'll meet him over the holidays. We were discussing weeping and the very fact that God has to break each of us before he can use us! And we were discussing the different confrontations we have had with Christ and what each one has done to our spiritual growth. And I thought about how you've shared with me those intimate moments when God has brought a river of tears to you—and whether they be of joy or repentance they have watered your spiritual tree of life and caused it to grow. Praise the Lord for the closeness of His very being to lift us to greater spiritual heights than we ever imagined possible.

I'm sitting in the back seat and I'm getting a little drowsy and as I was just relaxing I was thinking how blessed we are to be Christians. God is so real in this car as we've committed this trip to Him—and through the relationship of both of us to Christ, you are so near and real also because somehow I KNOW you're talking also to God at this very moment.

Because He lives!
Frances

*　*　*

Houston, Texas, November 29, 1969

Dearest Fran,

I feel like I have been plugged into a million volts

90

of electricity after receiving and devouring my Miami mail tonite!

You sure know how to create curiosity in a guy. In case I haven't told you, your books are the most exciting in the world, but being on the receiving end of your letters (and being a part of them right in the middle of events as they happen and written in such expression that my heart pounds faster), far exceeds the books (if that is possible) or am I just prejudiced or just something else?

Your card is now tucked away neatly in my billfold and on a floodlighted billboard in the curiosity chamber of my mind, which I couldn't stand much longer except that I'm aware of what happens when you receive two scriptures and wait for fulfillment. I would twist your arm except God might twist my neck for interfering with his timing of events, but whatever is in store, it will probably astound me when I know. And then you pour oil on the fire by whetting my appetite with your reference to Max Gaulke's comment—beautifully concealed (and there is no telling what he might say about me). And then for almost a total stranger who had spent a very busy week with a few hundred excited students and other kinds of people to conclude your whole week with a departing prayer, a peculiar one, but a prayer of your particular effective kind wondering about getting curves thrown by some unknown who or what which you were wondering about—and you really expect me to sleep tonite?! And then to put a delicious whipped-cream topping on the cake, Joan thrilled my heart with a very neat expression of what I hope is a westbound expression of the same kind of eastbound love I feel for her with *almost* enough "God Is Fabulous" stamps on the envelope surrounding her first letter to me, short tho it is. After hearing her answer the phone Wednesday nite after dashing in from a rainstorm with a very expressive "God Is Fabulous," I have fully concluded that she is a fabulous girl like you say she is!! I may just kiss her hello before I do you! I'll be looking forward to meeting your spiritual child Richard, but I probably won't kiss him.

Let's put our heads together over the holidays and figure an easier way to transport your books and records. Wish I could just carry them for you. Wait till you get sixteen books, which I believe is the number Joan suggested once upon a time.

I'll just phone Frances!

And I loved every single minute of our evening together on the telephone!

                              Yours truly (that will grab you),

It's just best not to put the complimentary close I might like to—but it's for sure that only God's way is the way we travel into our future—whether it's the way we think is right or not.

                                           Charles

P.S. Here's a mug shot of me enclosed that was snapped at my brother Milton's home at the lake.

*   *   *

Miami, Florida, Sunday evening,
November 30, 1969

Dearest Charles:

Just got home from church so thought I'd get busy

and write you a letter just sharing a few of the little goodies of the day.

Well, where do we start? Anyway, I think it's so funny that in spite of talking for two hours last nite (and it was about that long, wasn't it?) I still forgot half the things I wanted to say to you. Then I started laughing to myself and thought "I wonder how long we could go on without ever running out of things to say!" Then I decided we probably could have kept on until the wee hours of the morning or all night long, but it's better we ended it when we did, or you'd have to hock your plane ticket to pay for the calls, and we can't have that! I'll have to be honest and tell you, though, I dialed you this morning just before I left for Sunday School, but you must leave real early, because no one answered the telephone. I was just going to serenade you with a little song "I Woke Up This Morning With Heaven On My Mind (because I was thinking of you)" but guess the Lord knew best.

I watched the TV show we taped yesterday and I was amazed that they had really put the "youth" lens on, because I sure didn't look as baggy-eyed as I expected to after losing so much sleep, and then driving that little jaunt, but I'll have to be honest with you, even though I hate to admit it, I can see why people call me a sanctified Phyllis Diller—there's something about the way I laugh that sounds like her or something. Must remember to be more ladylike. Anyway, I had fun sharing the story of Christ on TV.

In my Sunday School class this morning I just shared some of the miracles of the convention and it was exciting. We prayed, cried, shared, and just had a fabulous time in general. By the way, the Sunday you have the class will be between Christmas and New Year's, but I'd like for you to save your testimony until New Year's Eve, unless you feel that God would have it otherwise. I just mention this, thinking that you might want to be collecting your thoughts for more than one "appearance." I wish you could see my date book which is all marked up—starting on the 23rd I have written CHARLES on the entire day and every day after that the same thing, until you have to leave to go home. (Might decide to kidnap you and keep you here forever!)

The day you get in will be our first Living Nativity Scene, so I think it's exciting one of the first places you'll get to go to is my church. By the way, your nephew was in my Sunday School class this morning —he usually teaches, but there he was this morning. I wonder if his dad mentioned anything to him about your coming? I haven't said a word to anyone except a couple of my very good friends and of course Joan is so excited! She was debating what she should call you—"Mr. Hunter," "Charles" or what. I told her not to be concerned, but just let the Lord direct her as to what she should call you.

We had such a thrilling service at church this morning. The pastor really "hung loose with Jesus" and it was just beautiful. Many of our young people had gone to the convention and had either accepted Christ or had rededicated their lives, and many more went this morning. I counseled with several at the altar this morning—and also with one of the entertainers at the Youth Convention. This one had gone up in the car with me. He really cried at the altar this morning—isn't it amazing that when you ride in a car with someone how God's Holy Spirit can convict you? And apparently from my unceasing conversation about Christ he felt a lack of total dedication in his own life. Praise the Lord! There were so many people who should have gone forward this morning, but who sit there thinking they're so saved and "sanctified" when they're really stupefied! The Spirit of God was so present this morning it was thrilling to watch those who listened. And in case you're interested, while I was there I prayed some special prayers for you, and also for me and also for us— prayers that the coming holiday season would be the most meaningful in our lives.

Well, after the last sentence I talked to you. I think I must have flipped my wig or something, because I keep thinking, "I'll call Charles just for three minutes." And then I say, "Lord, is that desire of you or the devil?" Then I say, "Get thee behind me Satan" . . . and believe me, if ever I should be tempted in any manner to have wrong thoughts about anything, that's all I have to do and God's Holy Spirit comes to my rescue, so I said, "Get thee behind me Satan" . . . (just checking out to see what the Lord had to say) and so I still thought, "I'll call Charles just for three minutes." So I did, so there!

Just stopped right there to read the 1st paragraph of James in the Phillips translation. (Now stop and think what I just said in the paragraph above.) And then I read what James says: "And if, in the process, any of you does not know how to meet any particular problem he has only to ask God—who gives generously to all men without making them feel foolish or guilty—and he may be quite sure that the necessary wisdom will be given him." All I can say is, "Thank you, Lord!"

I'll make the reservations for you tomorrow, so we won't have any problem with the holiday season, but we really don't anyway, because we're far enough away from all the "sin" activity of Miami Beach. By the way, if you can, why don't you make your flight early in the day. I asked Joan if she wanted to go with me to meet you at the airport, but she said to see if you couldn't come in early enough so I could pick you up alone, and then pick her up at school, but whichever flight you come on will be fine. Just let me know and we'll be there to meet you (and that "we" is just the Lord and me).

I hated to hear of you being pooped, and hope you got to bed real quick and got some Bible reading in. I'm sure you feel like I do—a real spiritual drought if you don't get Bible reading in. I know sometimes when I'm on tour I "give out" so much I am just spiritually drained when I get home. That's one of the reasons I believe the Lord lets me have an occasional trip where I don't share Christ with anyone, but instead just read His personal love letters to me . . . and that's the way I often feel about the Bible— real personal, and just for me. And Charles, I know how time consuming writing letters can be, and if ever it stands in the way of your reading the Bible, then make mine a real shortie, or just call me for three minutes and then spend your time in the Bible.

I'm going to write my Christmas letter sometime this week. I'll have to show you the other two I've written since the one was published. As I look at this past year, I can't believe what has happened and yet I'm not drooling over the past, I'm only excitedly looking to the future.

I'm enclosing the partial letter I wrote you in longhand. All I can say is I hope you can read it easier than I can, but I wanted you to know I was thinking about you anyway. In the event you can't read it, bring it to Miami and I'll translate it for you.

And I'm thinking you are real FABULOUS to loan your house out while you're gone. By the way, I'm sneaking parts of *The Saving Life of Christ* as I have time.

Goodnight, m'love, may the angels watch over you real good. Can't wait to see you.

In His great and abiding love,
Frances

P.S. Just dawned on me why you call me "Fran." You can't read my writing, because I really do write "Frances" out all the way, even though it doesn't look like it.

P.P.S. Two of the men from my church just called because they found out about Joan going to the hospital and they're coming over to pray for her healing. Isn't the concern of Christians magnificent?

*   *   *

Houston, Texas, December 1, 1969 (10:50 P.M.)

My dearest Fran,

Your call tonite was the most welcome and the most thrilling of all I have received from you—boy am I "xo"! ("relieved"!). You put everything at ease in my mind because now I feel very secure that with both of us committing everything to God with no plans of our own, then God will be able to give us his answer in a very definite way. That has been one prayer I have prayed with a definite request that his answer to both of us will be unmistakably clear—yes or no, but very clear and we will quickly accept whatever he says. I wonder what two scriptures are on your card in my wallet? I really loved every minute of your call!

Thank you, Lord God, for Tom's reactions! I know that he and Jan will be great Christians exactly when God is ready—and I'm anxious to be used, but above all I must speak only words furnished by the Holy Spirit—and he will speak the right words through someone. Sharpen Tom's appetite and we will feed him well on how God can be exciting to businessmen as well as his wonderful mother, also a business lady.

My mind has almost constantly been with Joan all day and all nite and she can be very sure I'll be praying for her tomorrow morning and I know we can trust God to do it his way which is the very best way, so she will be turned loose to Christ! Sure am anxious to know her.

I leave Houston on National Flight #184 on Dec. 23 at 1:30 P.M. and arrive Miami at 4:30 P.M. WOW! My heart beats faster just thinking about it.

I was in a client's office today (I had left *God Is Fabulous* and *Go, Man, Go* with the boss) and two customers were in her office and I let them know of two people who know how really fabulous God is and they want (and will get) your books. It is thrilling to see people suddenly speak out with either guilt or some event of their lives, and this time Helen said,

"Let me tell you a miracle in our family so you can tell some youth group . . .

"A few years ago a 16-year-old girl in Dallas (near Dallas) ran away from home with a not nice older young man. The family got the police looking for them. Helen and some others went to California for a vacation, I guess, and accidentally (?) got on a wrong (?) road and a car going in the opposite direction turned just at the time they were even with them and Helen said it was like God opened her eyes to see a license plate which seemed to stand out like a neon sign and she said, 'There they are!' They turned and pulled into a drive-in behind the girl's car and soon had her on a plane for home and now she is married to a very fine husband and settled down."

I told Helen the thrilling part of her story was that she recognized that God did open her eyes just as Christ said would be done and that she can be sure she had something great happen when God worked through her.

Sue came to see me at the office to return Keith Miller's *A Taste of New Wine* and we talked about twenty minutes. She has four beautiful teen-age children and is doing a marvelous job of raising them. Her husband died several years ago and she wants so much to do all of God's will and I feel is getting closer to turning loose to let God do it and not ask his help while she works for him. I'll admit God is a great assistant, but only when he is boss—in full charge—can his power come really alive. I'm going to take her to dinner, I believe it is next Tuesday (9th) and pray that God will speak through me to move her from one who works hard for him to one who rests in his joy, while he works through her. Hope you don't mind the way God chooses attractive ladies for me to witness to. You can be sure that is my only desire and God has full control. He really is powerful when he speaks through us with excitement. Sue went with us to the Yokefellow Convention a month or so ago.

I'll be anxiously awaiting your call tomorrow nite to tell me how very well Joan did and it will not come as a surprise from the Fabulous God Joan, you and I love and serve.

Love,
Charles

*   *   *

AUTHOR'S NOTE: Joan had an ear operation about four years prior to this time, but somehow the operation was not successful, and it became necessary for a second operation. I had talked to Charles about this on the telephone several times, and normally would have prayed and asked God's healing hand to touch Joan, but for some reason or other, this time I could not, and Joan (who always asks for divine healing for any ailment) could not accept the prayers of the men from the church who came to pray for her. This upset both of us, because we could not understand my reluctance to pray for my own child, nor could we understand her refusal to let someone else pray for her, but God had a special plan for us which we didn't know about at the time.

Joan went to the hospital on December 1st for the operation, and I kept a speaking date at a local

*church, running to the hospital as soon as I finished.
I stayed at the hospital the entire day, and because of
the necessity of far more extensive surgery than was
originally planned, Joan was under the influence of
the anaesthetic the entire day. I spent the whole day
reading God's word and sometime before noon a
dozen beautiful, long-stemmed, red roses arrived
with a beautiful card from Charles, and during the
long waiting period for Joan to return to reality, she
roused just long enough to look up for a moment,
and when she did, she saw the beautiful roses,
crooked her finger and uttered one word, "Charles?"
I said, "Yes," and she just smiled a beautiful smile
and went right back to sleep again. I sat and sat and
sat through the longest day of my life (so it seemed)
waiting for her to recognize me or to show some sign
that she was going to be all right, and the longer I sat
there, the more I realized that all my life I had had to
be "big mama" who took the kids to the hospital for
tonsils and adenoids, for impacted wisdom teeth, for
stitching when they had gotten hurt . . . I was the
"big mama" who took the neighbors' kids when they
got hurt . . . I was the "big mama" who went to the
funeral home with a young widow to select her husband's casket . . . and all of a sudden I didn't want to
be "big mama" anymore. Into my heart had come a
desire to cry on someone else's shoulder instead of
always having people cry on mine.*

*By 10:30 that evening the nurses and the physi-
cian assured me it was all right to go home, and I
flew home from the hospital, ran up the walk to the
house, opened the door as fast as I could, flew to the
bedroom where my telephone was, got out Charles'*

credit card number and called him up. The minute he answered the telephone with all the concern in the world, because he had undergirded me that entire day with prayer, I couldn't hardly say a word, because I had started crying and all I blurted out was, "Oh, Charles, I wish you were here!" Never had I felt so utterly feminine in my entire life—and never had I ever wanted someone to be with me to protect me in a time like this as I wanted Charles. I managed to bring myself under control and began telling him about the day and about the fact that Joan had said only one word during the day and that was Charles' name. Charles immediately sent Joan a wire after we finished talking which she received the next day, and also wrote a special delivery air mail letter to her.

We didn't know it at the time, but later on we understood why I hadn't been able to pray for her healing and why she refused to let others pray. God had a work to do in both of our lives, and he did it through this operation, because he used this time to win the heart of my 16-year-old Joan to the man who was to be her daddy, and he used this time to make me realize that I needed someone to love and protect me.

* * *

Miami, Florida
December 2, 1969

Dearest Charles:

HELP! I think I'd better go and visit the doctor tomorrow! The symptoms are most unusual and certainly not for a NUT my age. But I'm concerned about my irregular heartbeat which really galloped away when your picture fell out of the letter. Decided not to put it in my wallet, because I can't see it there, so have you sitting up on my desk so I can keep my eye on you while I'm writing to you. Even though the picture's a little dark, the expression is the expression of yours that I remember. Thank you so much for remembering I asked you for a picture. Can't wait to take you to the hospital in the morning so Joan can meet you.

I can't really believe that in just three weeks from tonight you'll be here and we'll be sharing in person instead of over the phone. You really have to pray that the Lord undergirds me on that Alabama trip so I'll keep my mind on my work and simmer down about the holidays. I was thinking about that today because as you said, my talks to God seem to really involve YOU these days, and then God gave me an exciting little thought which I'll pass on to you because He said, "With Christ living His life through you, would I give you a thought or desire that wasn't right?" And I had to honestly answer no because He's much smarter than I am.

Can't wait to see what He's going to do over the holidays. Who knows—maybe we'll write a book together. You said your plane would arrive at 4:30 P.M. Good. You remember I had asked you to come a little earlier in the day, but the Lord always knows best, doesn't he? Since I just get home the day before, I know I'll sleep a little later than usual because I AM exhausted when I return from a hard-hitting tour. I can catch up on my sleep, and also run to the store and to the cleaners and all those nonsensical things which MUST be done somehow or other, and then I'll be wide awake and beautiful (that's a laugh) and have everything ready so I can be there when your old plane comes in. Be sure and let me have the flight number, will you? I sure hope I have time to clean up this desk before you get here. It sure is a mess, but as long as I have room to write to you, I guess that's all right, isn't it?

I'm really enjoying Ian Thomas' book. He really has some great thoughts in it, doesn't he? The interesting thing is how God uses many people to write books and yet think how completely different we are in the way He uses us. Mine are so simple even a child can understand them, but I loved the inspiration I get from what Ian Thomas writes. He really shows deep thinking and I'm sure it takes him a lot longer to write than it does me.

By the way, I won't have time to do anything on *Hot Line to Heaven* before you get here, so maybe we'll go over it together if you'd like, so you can bring it with you if you want to and have plenty of time to go through it again before you give it back.

Charles, you've no idea how much I appreciate your genuine love and concern regarding Joan. Can't wait to get her comment about the card enclosed with the roses. And I was tempted to call you back and honestly tell you that her favorite flowers are red roses, but then I said, "Lord, I don't have to do that, do I, because You'll let him know, won't you?" And so you see, I wasn't the least bit surprised when they arrived this afternoon. They've got a beautiful big, big, big bow on the front of the vase that just matches the color of the roses perfectly.

. . . and because I can't say goodnight without

creating more curiosity concerning Max Gaulke's comment to me, you *should know what I said back to him.* So there!

All I can say is GOD IS FABULOUS. I'll never understand how He works, I only know that He does, and when He does a job, He does an excellent job. Goodnight, m'love, keep up those backup prayers.

In His most exciting love,
Frances

BANG . . . BANG . . . BANG . . . BANG . . . Just looked at your picture again . . . and that's my heart beating!

*   *   *

Miami, Florida, December 3, 1969
(IT'S NOW AFTER MIDNIGHT, SO IT'S ONLY 2 WEEKS AND 5 DAYS)

Dearest Charles:
Just finished talking to you and decided I'd better send you my schedule so you'll know where I am.

Friday, Dec. 5 Noon—Dade Jr. College
Friday, Dec. 5 to Sunday, Dec. 7, 11:37 P.M.—First Church of God, upstate Florida (don't even have the address)
Will call you Sunday night after I get home, which by the time I get my bags and get a cab home, will probably be around 12:30 or 11:30 your time. Please pray for this weekend as I understand this church has many problems, and I'm praying that our fabulous God will use me in a special way this weekend.

Wednesday night, Dec. 10—Westhaven Baptist

Church, Miami, Friday Noon, Christian Women's Club—Sweden House, Miami, Friday, Dec. 12 (Evening)—First Baptist Church, Lake Worth, Florida; Saturday, Arrive Huntsville, Alabama, Flight 669 at 8:08 P.M. (Sunday, Monday, Tuesday— Huntsville)

Wednesday, Dec. 17 (Day of prayer that the gals in Louisiana don't hijack you.)

Thursday, Friday, Saturday & Sunday—dates in Alabama given.

Monday (22nd)—Home at 11:54 A.M., madly rush around getting glamorous, etc. in preparation for GREAT day! (from 4:30 P.M. on). Tuesday (23rd), Wednesday (24th), Thursday (25th), Friday (26th), Saturday (27th), Sunday (28th)—Kendall Church of God. Monday (29th), Tuesday (30th), Wednesday (31st), Thursday (1st)—*Unavailable except for special appointments.* No phone calls, no work, no nothing, top secret priority work only. Rumor has it time will be spent in continuous P.T.L. conversation, prayer, etc. and all the things any non-Christian would think was nuts! (But we know, don't we?) Might even seriously consider attending various church services and Christmas functions at various denominations. Might even consider singing Christmas carols, might even consider having most fabulous ten days of my life.

God is so great, isn't He, Charles? I think of the peace and joy in your heart as you write a tribute to Jeanne and somehow your feeling in this has affected the way I feel about you because probably the greatest thing that comes through every letter and every thought and every phone conversation is the absolutely fantastic *agape* love that just oozes out of you, and I just say "Praise the Lord" for this. And I'm glad you feel the desire to finish it before Christmas, because I'm sure that God has spoken concerning this, too.

When I told you tonight how dumbstruck I was when I said, "So *you're* Charles Hunter!" I probably didn't convey what I meant so thought I'd better clear up the subject. When I said what I did, looked at you, and shook (or was I holding hands with you?) your hand I never in my entire life felt someone else's spirit bear witness with mine like yours did in a perfect blending, and it almost knocked me right off my feet. (I'm surprised I managed to talk that night.) I wonder if you realize how many thousands of people I have shaken hands with in the last year and how sensitive this has made me to those individuals whose spirits really bear witness with mine. A real blending comes only with another totally surrendered life, and so instantly I knew a lot more about you than you realized and frankly I had not anticipated your being so surrendered (I guess I was still thinking of you as a "dirty old man") and I guess it floored me.

Charles, a very, very special thank you for what you've done for Joan. She feels that very special quality of love that your every word imparts, and thank you for your love for Tom and Jan as well. I think it's real neat the Lord took me out of the house when you called so you could talk to him.

I can't help but think about the "fabulosity" of God as I look at your picture and realize that you could be spending the holidays with any young good-looking girl you wanted, and yet somehow or other God has chosen for you to spend it with me. I'll never understand *how* God works, but I'm grateful for the way He does.

Always, in His mighty love,
Frances

*   *   *

AUTHOR'S NOTE: The following letter was one of three waiting for me when I returned from the trip to upstate Florida. (Note the complimentary close.)

*   *   *

Houston, Texas, December 3, 1969

Dearest Frances,

So your name is really *Frances?* How do you do! In fact, nearly stranger of 60 days, it's good to know you. It still astounds me at the speed God is doing whatever it is he is doing with us—but I like it.

I'm glad Tom answered the phone tonite. He talks just like you. So many expressions are yours—and he sounds so energetic, even in spite of long hours of hard work. Each member of your family I *meet(?)* makes me more in a rush to speed by the next nearly three weeks. I believe Tom and I will get along great! In case he said something about me hesitating when he said who he was, I didn't realize I didn't even know his last name. Someway it sounded a little to me like your pastor's name and I was confused for a moment. Probably isn't anything like it.

You couldn't stir up my emotions more if I were a pot of soup and you used a big ladle because it really is an exciting joy to talk and talk with you. Wonder what my pink card scriptures are?

Guess what I just did! I reread your first two letters to me and my first to you. God must have written my invitation to the Party for the Lord in your second letter because you would have probably chickened out if you had waited to hear from me. Sure am glad! I notice I signed off "Love" and I'm almost afraid to now for fear my "carnal" heart might get the best of me, but I really am sure God is utterly dependable in arranging everything he plans for our lives. Speaking of keeping a guy curious, God has even outdone you, but he sure is working fast—20 days!

Wait till I tell you about the events surrounding today's exciting witness to the Jewish and Catholic couple. He really knows how to arrange unexpected (really I expect unusual ventures daily) appointments with strangers. I could hardly contain my excitement when I returned to the office. In fact I did share most of it with Dixie, the new lady accountant God sent us.

I xeroxed a copy of the letter Mama wrote me relating the great miracles and spiritual experiences she and Papa have had. It's a little hard to read, but when you have a few minutes you will thrill at what God has done for two people who have fully depended on God for nearly 40 years. I have been most fortunate to have them as parents. Their lives haven't been as exciting as yours and mine, but they were filled with His love.

I wish I could be there to help you do your nite

work which I kept you from so long tonite. I hope you don't have much more of long hours except the ones you spend for God in speaking. Maybe He will give you relaxing times in between.

It's bedtime so I had better slip away from you awhile, but not far away.

LOVE (I did it!)

Charles

*   *   *

Houston, Texas
December 4, 1969

Greetings, dear one,

Hurry and get off the phone so I can get you and not a busy signal! I really didn't expect to be able to wait till Sunday nite to talk with you. Nineteen days!

I wonder what words will fall on these pages which will be of interest to you.

Last nite was exceedingly nice—it always is when I get to talk with you. After that and after finishing your letter and after finishing Joan's letter I read a bit and got to bed about midnite thirty. At 5:30 this morning I woke up, got up and felt an urgency to get started right away—now what do you get started on right away at 6:30 A.M. when you just wake up from too short a nite? That's what I asked God and I put on a robe, went to the study and started writing, which I did for nearly three hours. I'm anxious to complete whatever it is I'm writing. I'll send it to you as soon as it's ready.

THEN OUR CALL . . .

How I wish words would flow from my mouth in

prayer like they do from yours, the very same thoughts you so beautifully expressed tonite were in my mind and heart. What a thrill it was as you were turning over to God so very completely the whole of our future and then you crowned your prayer with, "After all, YOU ARE GOD!" What a fabulous expression to God because you truly meant it! I would hate to be facing decisions that will be made by God in our lives; we can be perfectly at rest and know that he will decide each and every step we take either together or apart because "After all, you are God!" We need not expect anything less than the very best God has to give, which is much, much more than we can ever imagine or dream. You know—he's offering us his holy kingdom and we are accepting it which is the glory he expects from us. It's better to give than to receive, but he gives more than we are capable of receiving—all in a simple exchange for our worthless lives before he makes us so very rich!

You know, I don't really know if I love you in any way other than the tremendous love of God in our lives—I guess he is holding this kind of in reserve, because if he turned me loose no telling what would happen. It's exciting (boy, is it exciting!!) to have him taking every step in front of us and not telling us yet his plans! Maybe it's because his love is so great in our lives that it just completely overpowers any human love possible. Maybe there is no difference.

Pitter-Pat! (my heart!)

In whatever way he is arranging, I do love you,

Goodnite,
Charles

*   *   *

Miami, Florida, December 4, 1969

Dearest Charles:

Just hung up the telephone and I really do think we're both NUTS! How can any two individuals who don't know each other write constantly and then get on the telephone and blab incessantly and never run out of things to say and then have to sit right down and write another letter. I cannot understand it, and I never will. And you know it's peculiar, but when I talk to you, I feel utterly feminine. And for me that's really something, because I have had to work since I was 16 years old, except for 2 years, one when Tom was a baby, and one year when Joan was a baby, and it seems to me I've always had to compete in a man's world, and yet you say just "Hello" and I feel utterly feminine. (I think I must be cracking up!) . . . but if I am, just let me crack up! (I love it.)

It's real interesting what Tom said to me the other day when he asked me to tell him something about you, and the only thing I could think of was to tell him I knew nothing about you except that your soul was beautiful and that was all that counted. And I assured him that our relationship was Christ-centered and that was all. And for the classic remark of the century, he asked me: "Do you think Christ is enough?" I'm sure my teeth almost fell out (if I had false teeth that is) because all I could think of was, "Is there anything else?"

I was talking to a pastor this morning as I told you, about the tours, and something real interesting might develop from this. Somewhere in the conversation we became involved in marriage counseling and he shared with me what he shares with every couple contemplating marriage. And it was real interesting, especially when he drew a diagram on the reverse side. I'll try and draw one on another sheet for you.

I'm glad to know the old devil has been after you, too. I thought I was the only one he was after, because he was really using the old pitchfork on me today. Isn't it awful what it can do to you? I wasn't ever going to write to you or call you again, or anything. Truthfully, if I didn't believe in the Power of God, the old devil would have had a complete field day today! But P.T.L. I just called on the power of God's Holy Spirit and sent the old "debbil" running.

Well, right after that I got a phone call from Anderson. I almost had them call you. Do you remember I told you about the little girl with the curvature of the spine and the neck brace on and I was absolutely compelled to ask her if she would let me pray for her? They told me tonight the doctor was amazed—no braces are necessary. I couldn't believe some of the miracles I heard tonight, and I so wanted you to be on the phone listening with me because there's that urge to share everything with you, but I refrained from having them put you on the line too. Also talked to one of my special loves, Rev. Dave Grubbs (do you know him?). And talking about special loves—you asked me tonight if I'm not jealous when you take these other women out to dinner. Not the least bit, not the least bit . . . I'LL JUST SCRATCH THEIR EYES OUT WHEN I SEE THEM. That's all. (In a Christian way, of course.) Honestly, if I were real truthful, I'd say for a brief moment I

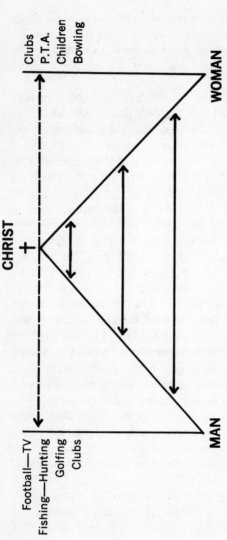

Football—TV
Fishing—Hunting
Golfing
Clubs

MAN

CHRIST

WOMAN

Clubs
P.T.A.
Children
Bowling

With Christ the Center of the home, man and woman eventually become **one** as the Bible says. Note the diagram forms a "W" to indicate the things of the world which draw a couple apart. Christ is the only person that permanently brings a man and a woman closer to each other. Temporarily other interests may bind, but eventually take apart as diagram shows! NEAT?

return to living in the "flesh" where jealousy is a reality, but then I remember just as quickly that in God's beautiful love there is no jealousy and that's where I prefer to stay wrapped safe and secure in God's love. But nevertheless, I'll be sending fiery darts to Houston next Tuesday. So there!

I put National Flight No. 184 in my date book with a real special "blob" around it for the 23rd of December. I can't believe it's so close, and yet I can't believe it's so far away. Two weeks and 5 days (nope only 4—it's after midnight). Ooops, and just as I wrote that, I almost panicked and decided to leave town on the flight which leaves at 4:29.

I'm so glad that Rich is going to be here the whole holiday season. I'll see if he wants to stay at the motel with you. I can only warn you, he'll talk your arm off. He's so exciting, though, and without a doubt, my strongest booster.

And did you say you heard they were asking me to come to Houston February 5th? I looked at Max Gaulke's letter and I gathered it would be the following week, when I can't go to Houston. I'll write him real quick, because I'd have to get some speaking dates in the other churches, because they have no allowance for honorariums or travel expenses, and said the only thing they could offer was room and board. Just happened to remember, I'll have my royalty check by then.

No more until Sunday night—I'll call you just as soon as I get back home. Remember to really keep me in your prayers, and remember to keep "us" in your prayers, too, for God's perfect will. Two little verses of scripture keep coming to my mind because when the Lord told me to memorize them, I memorized them!

Goodnight, my love, may the wonder and power of God's great love surround you as you read this letter. As I sit here typing it, I am completely engulfed with His presence. It's at moments like this I feel almost the physical need to put my arms heavenward, which somehow or other communicates "surrendered" to me.

In His love,
Frances

*   *   *

December 5, 1969, Miami, Florida, A.M.

Dearest Charles:

Almost forgot I had a noon speaking date and haven't even picked up my airline ticket yet and must leave here all packed by 1:30.

Just wanted to let you know that your picture is safely anchored in my Bible, which I take everyplace I go. (And I open it more than I do my wallet, so it makes it better this way.) More en route. . . .

(En route) After speaking this morning, removed your picture from Bible! Too distracting when I opened it to read something—put you in date book instead. Will return you to Bible when I'm reading alone, but I think I missed a couple of words because my heart skipped a beat!

Please note postmark: Houston. I'll never tell how it happened to be mailed there! (Oh, I gave the letter to the stewardess to mail in Houston.) Stewardess

116

and husband are reading my books; pray for lightning to hit!

Much love because of Him,
Frances

*   *   *

Upstate Florida, Friday night, December 5th, 1969

Dear Charles:

Since I used up the one envelope I had with me, I borrowed some paper to let you know I'm thinking of you.

Wasn't the postmark "neat" on that last letter? Don't you think I'm a smarty to get a letter to you so quickly? When I got on the plane, I had no idea the destination was Houston, and when I found out, I almost stayed on all the way. I was only on the plane for 30 minutes, so didn't have an opportunity to share much.

The pastor's wife had a real reawakening about 2 years ago and is on fire, but I sure didn't see much fire anywhere else. As a matter of fact, I didn't even see any smoke—all I could see was dead, dead ashes. Sometimes I feel it would be better and easier to go out and win all new people to the Lord than to try and break through the old "saved and sanctified" Christians. Ugh. . . .

Tomorrow a breakfast, luncheon, youth dinner and evening service.

I'm really praying the Lord will do some exciting things during the holidays. I'm praying that Tom will look at you as a businessman because this is what he really needs to see. I'm going to even be willing to disappear for a *little* while so you can talk to him as

117

the Lord leads. And then I'll have to turn around and pray the Lord doesn't lead you to talk to him too long.

I opened my date book to your picture which is right above where I have your card stapled in my book and I looked around the room for a telephone—so it's a good thing there's none here or the phone company would have made some more money.

No more tonight—I'm exhausted—the church has no mike, so I really strained my voice.

12/6—Saturday afternoon. What a day and how I wish I could talk to you and share the day with you. I have such an uncontrollable desire to share every moment of joy and of defeat with you!

The breakfast this morning was unreal! They were still DEAD! When I came out into the car I really cried out and said, "God, *wake them up!!!*" Sometimes I wonder why God has called me to a church.

The women's luncheon was good and the response was excellent, BUT it was right in the middle of a New England Oyster House, NO PRIVACY at all. So I spoke to all the outsiders, too, some of whom will be at the service tonight.

Thank you for your prayers, Charles. Just resting safe and secure in the knowledge that you are praying too helps no end. Even as I sit in this room miles from you, I know that God unites our spirits! And it's amazing as I realize how close He brings you to me even though there is a big hunk of land between us.

Am gonna lay down for a few minutes before tonight. I'll share with you by phone what the Lord had me do this afternoon and why I'm so exhausted! P.T.L. Saturday night: (Fleeting thought—wonder if

I could sneak out to the phone and make a call. Better not—especially when I realize my host and hostess are sorta related to you!)

I called home tonight and talked to Joan. She said I had the fattest letter from you I've ever gotten and she was so amazed I had forgotten to leave my phone number there because she wanted to call me and let me know I had mail from you. I was going to take a cab home tomorrow night from the airport, but she said, "I'll pick you up, Mother, so you won't have to wait for your letter." Isn't she a doll?

After all the weeping I did today for this congregation we finally had a real breakthrough tonight. The altars and front pews were filled. It really shakes me up when people don't respond to God's Holy Spirit. Tomorrow A.M. I have the teens at Sunday School, Morning Worship, Training Class on Winning Souls at 3 P.M. Evening service and then home *and a telephone call to you.*

As I sit here with your picture watching me write to you, I just Praise the Lord for how close He brings you to me. And I really praise Him for giving us the exciting relationship He has. And another BIG P.T.L. for telephone calls. I hope I can stand waiting to talk to you. Ugh . . . No more tonight—want to pray—and must read my Bible.

Because of His love, I love,
Frances

Sunday A.M. The pastor just brought my coffee into my bedroom—WOW—such service! I'm not used to this.

I'm reading my Bible—just claimed the promise

that: "All things are possible to him who believes!"
NOTHING is impossible to God.

P.T.L.

*   *   *

Houston, Texas, Saturday, December 6, 1969

Dearest Frances,

Want to hear something really exciting. Especially it's exciting how God's Holy Spirit reaches both of us about the same subject. As I read the second paragraph of your letter (12/4) about your conversation with Tom—"Do you think Christ is enough" and "Is there anything else?"—I was so overflowing with the presence of the Holy Spirit that I cried, and you know how wonderful that is! Then in your last paragraph you said, "May the wonder and power of God's great love surround you as you read this letter. As I sit here typing it, I am completely engulfed with his presence." The rest of your letter also was thrilling, but you see, your prayer was registered and was answered before I read your parting comment, and this marvelous, thrilling power of God was flowing again through both of us—and if that isn't great enough, it started with our love for Tom and there it will continue to flow till Tom, too, can say, "Is there anything else!"

Last nite I had dinner with a young couple and God's food was even better than the lovely dinner she had prepared. I really love those two kids! You know, we concluded our visit at 2:30 this morning with a three-party circle of prayer with Christ in our midst (where two or three are gathered in my name, there am I in the midst of them), and with the Holy

Spirit present in a very keen sense, we asked God to help these wonderful young people to "turn loose" and let God have all of their lives—and they so want this. The wife said she was made so aware of her failure to be serving Christ right because the devil hadn't been bothering her at all lately. She said, "I think I made the devil happy today; I think he was well pleased with me." And then you said in your letter, "I'm glad to know the old devil has been after you, too!" Let's all of us together drive him away from all of us—and we do know he can't win when God, and not us, is at war with him.

Oral Roberts sent me a plaque which sits upright on my desk like a calendar which, with your picture fastened above it says:

Frances'
Picture

SOMETHING GOOD IS GOING TO HAPPEN TO YOU

Thanks for sending me your picture—it is much more personal than the publicly shared ones. I can get happy just looking at it—a million dollar smile, because it comes from the treasury of God's kingdom in your heart! Seems I've seen you someplace before. I must meet you personally someday—in sixteen days for instance. Wonder what God has in mind for us.

I've been constantly with you in my prayers and know you have had some more fabulous experiences which God is giving you, not just for your pleasure, but for speaking and writing about his power so it will reach many thousands from now till eternity!

Please don't catch the 4:29!

Love,
Charles

* * *

AUTHOR'S NOTE: My daughter's recovery was excellent, so I took her down to my daughter-in-law's house to stay for the weekend since she didn't want me to cancel my trip, and I left for upstate Florida. The plane I was on made one stop in Florida, and then the next stop was Houston, Texas. My human heart wanted so badly to stay on the plane, and yet I knew I had to be where God called me to be, so I wrote a real quickie note on the plane, gave it to a stewardess to mail in Houston, and got off at my appointed stop.

This was a most unusual and interesting weekend. Somehow I couldn't get my mind off of Charles. It seemed that everything in my life concerned Christ, God, and Charles, and yet somehow or other I was tormented—my stomach was upset, and I couldn't really straighten out all my thoughts because I knew that I was so in love with someone I only knew by letters and telephone calls, but I believe that God put me in the church that he did for a very special reason. This happened to be a real DEAD, DEAD church (ever been in one?). The more I talked about the fabulosity of God, the more they said it was impossible for things like this to happen in their church. The more I talked about the great things that God

*was doing in other churches, the more convinced
they were that it was impossible in this town. I went
to a men's breakfast on Saturday morning, a wom-
en's luncheon on Saturday afternoon, a series of in-
dividual calls later on, but everything was completely
negative. I believe I cried more tears this weekend
than I ever have over any church. They were so convinced everything was impossible that I was miserable.*

*Between the problems in the church, and my per-
sonal problem about refusing to admit that anything
was possible in my own life concerning love, romance, or marriage, I was about as miserable as I've
ever been in my life. It seemed the more negative the
church got, the larger the problems in my own personal life became. By Sunday morning I was in a
thundering mood. Now I don't thunder very often,
but when necessary, and God says to do it, I really
thunder, and I began thundering on Sunday morning.
With all of my available lung power I screamed at
them, "NOTHING IS IMPOSSIBLE TO GOD. . . .
NOTHING, NOTHING, NOTHING!" I was desper-
ate because I knew they HAD to be awakened
from their sleep if anything was ever going to happen in their personal lives and in the life of the
church. About the third time I yelled the word
"Nothing"—do you know who was convicted? I
WAS! There I was standing telling them that
NOTHING was impossible to God, and yet I was
telling God that in my own life, love, marriage and
romance was an impossibility.*

*I was never so shocked at myself in my entire life
as I was in those moments when God's Holy Spirit*

convicted me. I guess I gave the shortest altar call in the history of any church. I merely said as fast as I could get the words out, "If you've got a problem, bring it to the altar, and God will answer it!" And I immediately left the pulpit, and practically jumped over the altar rail to be the first one there. I simply laid Charles Hunter on the altar. In absolute agony I cried out, "God, what do you want out of my life? And what has Charles Hunter to do with my life?" And then I screamed silently in misery and said, "God, let me know what to do with him, or if he has no place in my life, GET HIM OUT OF MY MIND, MY THOUGHTS, AND MY HEART!"

Immediately a peace flooded my soul, and while I didn't know the answer, I knew that God had answered my prayer. Immediately after the service concluded, I went back to the parsonage, into my bedroom and laid down to read my Bible, because somewhere in this book I knew I would find the answer that God had for me. The Bible opened to the 6th chapter of Matthew and my eyes fell on the 33rd verse: "But seek ye first his kingdom and his righteousness, and all these things shall be yours as well." I backed up to the 25th verse and read: "Therefore I tell you, do not be anxious about your life. . . ." GOD HAD SPOKEN . . . He had been trying to tell me that because I had sought first the Kingdom of God and his righteousness, "all" these things would be added, and one of the things he was adding to my life was Charles. God was saying, "I want to give you someone to love you, to protect you, to cherish you for the rest of your earthly life because you have put me FIRST in your life." I sobbed and said, "Thank

*you, Lord, thank you Lord!" Never from then on
was there any turmoil in my heart and soul concerning Charles. I just simply said, "Lord, what shall I do
now?" and in the beautiful way that God has of telling us the next step, I knew INSTANTLY what to
do. I flipped out of bed as fast as I could, grabbed a
piece of notebook paper, and on it in firm bold letters I simply printed the following message:*

December 7, 1969
Upstate, Florida

I

LOVE

YOU!

*I was a real spiritual chicken, because I didn't sign
that letter, but a peace flooded my entire body and
mind as I wrote those three magic words on the
paper as God had told me to! In other words, I had
been obedient to God, and as a result, the turmoil
was gone. I addressed an envelope to Charles, tucked
the letter on the inside and put it in my pocketbook
to mail it at the airport when I left town to return
home that night. Note that the three letters from
Charles which were waiting for me from my trip said
"LOVE." God had moved in on both of us the same
weekend. I received the three letters at the same time
Charles received my letter which had just the three
words on it. (I wonder what happened as the air-*

planes crossed in the air . . . they probably backed up and gave each other a big kiss.)

As soon as Charles received the unsigned letter (there was no doubt in his mind who the letter was from) he called me and without any prefacing remarks at all, said, "Honey, when can we be married?" I immediately replied, "Let me look at my date book!" Many people might think this was a peculiar way to answer, but after all, my life was really controlled by a date book because of all the commitments I had made to churches and other religious organizations. I looked at the book and said, "1969—nope; 1970—nope; 1971. . . ." and realized by this time that God himself would have to plan our wedding date, because I couldn't see any possible time in my schedule when we could get married.

There are many who might say, "Well, why not cancel some of the dates in your book?" Well, if you must know the truth, both Charles and I knew that I could not cancel a date to go to a church where God had called me, and I knew that since marrying Charles was part of God's plan for my life, that God would have the entire solution already worked out if I would just listen to him. After again looking through my date book for the next two years I decided right then and there that God would have to do it all, so Charles and I decided to pray and seek God's guidance and leading.

One of the things that Charles did ask, however, was when my daughter Joan would be out of school. I answered that school would be over the first week in June. Charles had replied that maybe we could be married in June, but I didn't tell him that as soon as school was out Joan and I were going to the International Convention of the Church of God for one week, and from there to Detroit, and from there to a youth camp for a week, and from there to churches in the Chicago area, and there was the month of June all gone. I just said to this comment, "Let's pray about it!"

* * *

Houston, Texas, Sunday, December 7, 1969 (2:30 P.M.)

Dearest Frances,

God, please let me capture on paper what my choir director and his wife just said, even though he said he didn't really remember just what he said. And it is plain that the Holy Spirit was speaking a tremendous truth.

Frances, I just had dinner with our choir director, his wife and one of the tenors. Ray was commenting that the spirit of unity in the tenor section was inspiring. Then Ray and Betty began intertwining their thoughts into something that struck me with a sense of awe! I mentioned to Ray about relating to you what he said about the freedom of the voice when it was turned loose and about you being impressed with this. Then he advanced the thought, with Betty's support, that for just short periods when they were studying music under a great musician, they reached a release in their voices which was so spiritual that it was as if their voices began to float in a freedom like it was only encased in a housing or temple but floated independently of this housing in which it was contained. He said it was a marvelous, awesome spiritual freedom of release, which is I'm sure one of the reasons for his use of the expression "turn loose" of your voice and it operates in the freedom in which God made it.

This is what you and I have felt in being able to turn loose of ourselves and let God have this floating freedom as if he is detached from our physical bodies, yet within our spirits, only contained within a housing, the temple of God. I hope this marvelous revelation communicates with you in the way it did to me as Ray was talking.

This led me to relate to them the way the power of God flows through us when we can find just that spark of trust to let him have his freedom to use us. So many times God has events occur three times because under the Jewish Law, two witnesses agreeing could prove a point of law and God added one to leave no doubt. When God the Father, Son and Holy Spirit agree with our spirit all the power in the universe and heaven is available. The third sensation of floating freedom came to me two or three years ago while I was in the last week of an Evelyn Wood Dynamic Reading Course. One nite as I was practicing reading using the method developed by Mrs. Wood, I was reading 1200-1500 words per minute and a tenseness in the front area of my brain developed from pushing for speed with comprehension, when suddenly all pressure released and it was like my mind began floating and like the reading was being poured into my mind. On the bulletin board area of our choir room is a poster which states in effect that your music must originate in your mind and by thinking the music your voice sings it.

Look how the spirit of your mind is the heart of all three sensations of floating freedom (1) turning loose of yourself in total trust in God acting; (2) turning loose of your voice and (3) turning loose of your mind to let reading freely pass from printed pages through your eyes which are the windows to your mind. There is little telling what else we are binding which, if it were released to God, would be as fabulous as the simple trust which has brought to you the reality of God through your experiences. For instance, science is working now on fast hearing which I'm sure can be released when man understands or when God wants him to. It's not the speed I'm excited about—it's the floating freedom unbound by time and spontaneous without effort on our part and is impossible when we try to create it through our effort. It all comes from turning loose to let God use his power. The little calls for God to come to your rescue when you get in a tight spot are not limited by time and God's replies have no time limitations when his plan is being directed through us.

10:40 P.M. Just an hour till I'll be talking with you, and barely over two weeks till I'll be in mmmmmmmmm! My travel plan instructions are most interesting—"From Houston to Christian Love-in"!!¡¡ (Spanish punctuwowshun mark¡¡) It sure had a lot of information which I'm glad has a lot of loving meanings. I wonder if I fully understand "Prepared by FG in accordance with divine instructions" and on another letter with picture enclosed "Here's someone who knows something you don't know." I'm anxious to know what the other side of your secret really is! But most of all I'm glad you (and I) can't wait and the devil has fle - flee - flea-d—don't let him hang around just because he is pilot of the 4:29.

I just glanced up and saw Jeanne's picture on my desk (a small picture on a glass paperweight) and nearby your picture, and felt complete harmony in my heart about all that is happening. God has so completely and perfectly taken care of any feelings that probably would normally exist and it's really marvelous that all is well in that department. Now just one statement hit my mind which I haven't thought of in a long time. Jeanne knew apparently beyond any doubt that she would not live and seemed to be completely satisfied that God was taking her, and sometime within two weeks of her death she said, "You are free" and I said, "What do you mean" and she said, "Free to marry again." At one time many months or years before she had stated that if she died first I shouldn't remarry. God so completely absorbed her in his love that just as it had been a perfect marriage it ended in a perfect death, a happy death. If I didn't know God and his gifts to me, I would think the end of the last sentence above was impossible, but whatever God does, he really does a total job.

Can it really be possible that as I look at your picture God is letting me fall in love?

Goodnite,
Charles

P.S. I was rereading this letter and remembered as I read "binding" and "released" that when you wrote

130

three words which I will receive by Tuesday you were released from being bound.

Fabulous

* * *

Miami, Florida, December 8, 1969

Dear One (or my big bowl of soup):

Just a real quickie note because it's 2:30, and I promised Tom I'd come in for a little while today. Just took Joan to the doctor and he took two of the stitches out and says it looks fine. I'm so glad the big burden of it is all over.

We stopped at the Howard Johnson's on the way home and they don't have any rooms available for New Year's and Christmas. Well, P.T.L. Came home and immediately called the Holiday Inn which is about 5 miles further up the road, but which is probably nicer, and got a reservation there.

And what does that P.T.L.V.E. on the envelope mean? Bill Ellis on his newsletter wrote PTLEOMM (Praise the Lord Even On Monday Morning)—how 'bout that?

Enjoyed talking to you last night even if my daughter did almost give you a heart attack by saying I wasn't home. I think we're a couple of real nuts that we can just keep blabbing without regard to the amount of time or anything else. Can't wait for you to get here so that I can think of an hour as a short period of time instead of a long period like I do now.

Your letters are so absolutely beyond the human ability to write, I read them over and over again, and love them more each time I reread them. I think Joan enjoys them as much as I do, and she really got a charge out of the pot of soup-ladle routine! (So did I.) Rich called today. He's coming home on the 21st. I'll be home on the 22nd, and you'll be here on the 23rd. Can't wait. Can't wait. Can't wait. Can't wait. Can't wait.

More tonight, but in the meantime, didn't want a day to slip by without something from the ladle. After all, you might forget me if I do.

Truthfully, the main reason I wanted to write you was to tell you to PLEASE PLEASE PLEASE PLEASE do not even consider spending anything in the way of Christmas presents for me or my family. This trip is going to cost you a small fortune as it is and the only thing I want for Christmas is to see you safely here. I'm sure the Lord knows just sharing this most wonderful season of the year with you is better than anything else he could give me (having already given me the abundant now and eternal then—life). I've been trying to figure out where in the Bible the Lord promises all these extra BIG blessings, but I'm grateful. When Rich was talking to Joan today and also to me, he said, "I can't imagine you responding to anyone like you are!" My only comment . . . when the Lord does something, he takes all the little details into consideration. AMEN.

In the meantime, I read the letter from your mother and they've really had some exciting miracles in their lives, haven't they? You could just feel her love of God coming right through the letters.

Joan just reminded me that we all have the same middle initial—"E." I told her that was for ETERNAL. How 'bout that? Behave yourself with all those gor-

geous women now, but as long as it's for the Kingdom of God, GO, MAN, GO!

In his exciting wonder what
He's going to do next service,

Frances
(or the big ladle)

P.S. The Oral Roberts' Christmas Show sounds
great!! We'll watch it.

*   *   *

Miami, Florida, December 8, 1969

Dearest Pot of Soup:

If you don't think I have a problem with myself,
you'd better think again! Every time I sit down to
write some of the zillions of letters I have to write,
God always seems to remind me that I really ought
to take time out to write to you first, so I just let
some of the rest of the letters go down the drain.

Well, here it is three hours later and three telephone calls—one with Herb Streeter and the other
two with you, and all of them have thrilled me to
death. I do hope you will really keep Tom in your
prayers during this most critical time.

I'm so excited at the prospect of seeing you in
February, just a little over a month after you'll be
here for the holidays. I think it's so neat that little
part of my schedule was open. Yipes, and that just
reminded me—I've got to buy a coat before I go to
Alabama, because someone up there told me it was
20 degrees last week, and I'll freeze to death in that
temperature.

I'm wondering how I'll last through the next two

weeks. It's been so great talking to you so extravagantly on the telephone, and then all of a sudden to realize I won't be able to talk to you is a revolting thought! Well, I'm just going to pray that somewhere along the line I'll find a phone with enough privacy that I can sneak in a little call to you. I'm sure the Lord will find someplace during that time when I can have a couple of words with you anyway, even if it isn't a long call.

I just turned to my Phillips translation and read what you had read to me over the telephone, and I backtracked to James 1:13—"A man must not say when he is tempted, 'God is tempting me.' For God cannot be tempted by evil, and does not himself tempt anyone." And all I could think of was how many times Satan has tempted me with thoughts of disbelief concerning our relationship (he tells me I'm too old, too!), and in case you're interested, he's also tempted me with thoughts of "what would you do without all those people clamoring to shake your hand and who just want to touch you because they think that will make their own relationship to God more exciting?" . . . and then as soon as I have told him to get thee "hence" those doubts disappear because I know that nothing is impossible for God. It's just a question of HOW He's going to do WHATEVER He's going to do!

I'm going to send out a little blurb to my Sunday School class telling them that we'll have a distinguished guest from Houston teaching our class, and see if I can't encourage each of them to bring a couple of guests. Now that will be a switch, won't it? Me sitting down like a quiet little mouse and letting you do all the talking. Well, fair is fair . . . you listened enough to me in Houston.

We'll discuss more in detail where I'll be staying in Houston, but let's don't forget that because we are both well known as Christians, we could never do anything that would cause our brother to stumble. *You* and *I* know that I could stay in your home since you have a Christian housekeeper, with no concern at all as to what God would say, but how would this affect someone whose relationship to Christ was not as strong. That's the only thing that concerns me and I know that neither of us would ever be in a situation that would be detrimental to the cause of Jesus Christ, but again, here's a situation we'll just put in the Lord's hands and I know He'll find the answer for us.

I was just thinking of that song " 'Tis So Sweet to Trust in Jesus." I don't think I ever actually appreciated those words before right now, but that really is true, isn't it? I told them yesterday at Vero Beach that I always felt like I was sitting in a big innertube just floating around in the ocean, completely relaxed, because God was making all the decisions.

Well, my luv, it's time I signed off and poured my Miss America body into bed, or I should say, my Grandma America body into bed. Anyway, whatever it is, I'm tired, but knowing that in just a few days I won't be able to use the typewriter, I wanted to get off as much as I could in advance. However, I'll be scribbling notes along the way in longhand, but you know, God really knows best, doesn't He? Because

think how exciting it will be to see you on the 23rd—
even more so, because I won't have had the opportunity of talking to you for a short time previously.

Thanks for your prayers, Charles, thanks for your thoughts, and thanks just for being you because of Him. I'm glad I didn't know you when you were a nasty old sinner. Aren't you glad you didn't know me? I am!

He lives and loves,
Frances

P.S. Next morning: Between Jesus Christ and Charles Hunter, I sure don't seem to think or talk about anything else!

*　*　*

Houston, Texas, Wednesday 7:45 A.M.
December 10, 1969

Dearest WOW!

Last nite's neat little three-minute talk was just right. I went right to bed when we finished talking and calmly was too excited to sleep!

This morning I woke up at 6:45 and realized this was Wednesday and time for our men's prayer breakfast, so I dashed away after slightly dressing and was at church at 6:55. The devotion is at 7:00.

I have an 8:30 appointment downtown so I'd better get ready to disappear, but just had to say Good Morning to a special someone.

13 DAYS!!!!!!!!!!!!!!!!!!!

Love that daily increases,
Charles

Houston, Texas
December 10, 1969

I

LOVE

YOU!

X (my mark)

Still December 10, 1969
December 10, 1970 ?!!!

Dearest Sweetheart,

Yours truly,
Charles

'Fraidy cat! Don't you trust God, Charles?

Sure I do, and now I'm finding a new release altho
He was making His way clear. Now it's brighter and
very cheery! I like it!! Much!!

The predominant thought is—by both of us trusting God how can 1970 be less than fantastically
fabulous!

I just opened Phillips to Philippians 3rd and 4th
chapters and the first underlined words I saw were
"and remember how much I love you." If Paul can
write it to the Philippian Church so can I as part of
God's blessings write it to you. And then, "Don't
worry over anything whatever; (like whether God is
actually arranging our lives his way) tell God every

137

detail of your needs in earnest and thankful prayer, and the peace of God, which transcends human understanding, will keep constant guard over your hearts and minds as they rest in Christ Jesus." And we really are amazed at how we have sat on the sidelines and watched Him really work fast, with perfect timing and magnificently! How can we ever thank God for picking us out of a few billion people and planning what we can be sure will be an unbelievably exciting and loving life of bliss in serving him and feeling his tremendous power flowing through our lives. It's really a tingling thrill to just peek into 1970 and see us together with him, and from here I really can't see any specific arrangement—it's a surprise known only by God which makes it even more exciting. Hope you can sleep tonite!

I guess you can tell, this is the first time I've felt really free and honest to say with all my heart, "I do love you, Frances!" And the only way I can possibly say it is by a "wreckless" trust in God. You realize this is the biggest decision in our personal relationship and it's being made with absolute lack of knowledge by either of us about the other—Boy! this is really trusting in God, and we don't have to worry over anything whatever! In case you don't notice, I'm tingling tonite with the thrill of the Holy Spirit in full command of our ship!

And if God will so abundantly bless our lives, think of the effectiveness it will have on others because we can never look selfishly at our blessings when his main purpose in teaming us as partners is for reaping a harvest of souls for him and glorifying

Him by our totally dedicated service for the rest of our lives.

WOW FOR GOD!

You and God really made me happy tonite and I hope and believe you are truly mixed up in this ter-rific triangle of love and I'm glad the third side of this triangle is God!

Bedtime—hope you are sleeping soundly by now!

Sweet dreams,

I love you,

Charles

PTLVE means "Very Especially."

* * *

Miami, Florida, December 10, 1969

Dearest Charles:

I was so wound up after talking to you last nite for over two hours (P.T.L. for whoever invented the telephone) that I don't think I got to sleep until around 5:00 this morning, but I really crack myself up when I get that way. I keep saying, "Lord, how can this be?" And then God just wraps me in His arms of love around yours around me and that realllllly finishes me off.

By this time you will have received my three-word letter—and all I could think of after I had mailed it was what most of the advertisements they print about me say: "A hard-hitting speaker, who tells it like it is!" AMEN! I hope a holy hush doesn't fall on you after such holy boldness (and that's really saying something, isn't it?) but believe it or not, I've no feeling of being bound any more. SO THERE.

Your letter of this morning thrilled me to death for

many reasons. First of all, because your letters always *grab* me. My heart doesn't simmer down all day long and every time I look at the envelope my heart really reacts! Never had so much fun in my life—or should I say JOY, because there's a real big difference between the two.

Second, your letter thrilled me with your remarks concerning Jeanne. I think it's most unusual that there has never been any feeling of anything except how fortunate she was to have had you for a husband and to have been your wife. I've read in the lovelorn columns, which I used to read before I became a Christian, of the tremendous jealousy people have for the previous wife, and yet I feel she had a tremendous influence on the kind of a person you are now and your attitude toward me, and so I'm glad you have "harmony" as you put it, about two women in your life. Do you remember what I prayed concerning this the night I last saw you? I do, and I also remember what you said.

I've got to really run, I don't know how I could possibly have the urge to write you 9 million pages after all the blabbing we did last night, but seems like I never run out of exciting things to share with you, but most important, I never run out of the *desire* to share everything with you.

Gotta share one thing. I still don't have any Christmas shopping done—absolutely no time. I did get Jan a camera (movie) for Christmas which I gave her early, and I bought my grandbaby a beautiful high chair which he also needed early, but I'm sure I'll think of lots of other things I can get for them, although as I think I said in a previous letter, becoming a Christian has certainly changed my ideas concerning Christmas.

I absolutely feel so completely overwhelmed at the thought of the holiday season, it's unreal. I talked to Gene Cotton today—I didn't want him to be floored at anything the Lord might come up with, and I didn't want him to even hear any rumors from anyone else. I wish he and his wife could be here for Christmas because they are two people who have Christ, and nothing else in their marriage. And as Gene said today: "Who needs anything else?" And I said a big AMEN.

My prayer for the whole world is that they would know the real joy of living and loving that Christ has given to us. Never in all my Christian life (and certianly not my non-Christian life) have I ever felt the blessings from God as I do approaching this holiday season.

FOREVER in His love,
Frances

* * *

AUTHOR'S NOTE: Every telephone call that Charles and I have ever had with each other has always ended with prayer. Probably one of the best investments we ever made was in the money we spent to pray with each other over the long-distance telephone. The night of December 11th our prayers were for God to make the arrangements for the wedding because we didn't know when we could possibly get married.

* * *

Houston, Texas—

11:40 P.M. my time
12:40 A.M. your time
My time is your time
12-11-69

My sweetheart,

What a beautiful prayer you just prayed—it just wrapped in a real neat package what we both are so thankful to God for giving us and with this just the beginning, but we both know that our joy can only exist together because His love is really going to others through us and because it's His running water of life, it's fresh and great, but if it stopped in us then it would become instantly dead, and this must never happen. How can this awesome sense of the power he is investing in us as a unit be described. I feel that something almost as big as the creation of the universe is about to happen, and it is that same power which created the universe that we feel within us. Yes, we trust God to make every decision we face—so far no effort or concern—ultimately no effort or concern because we rest in the love of Christ Jesus.

It's interesting the sensation that comes from releasing a balloon into the air and watching it float away and it's gone, but we have for no other reason than trust in God, released our whole lives to him; even before we had a first date to say: "God, you have planned that we become one for you, so here, God, are our lives. You plan the whole wedding, even when and where it will be and we will instantly respond because you always let both of us know

142

when you speak to us. The very fact that this is the most important event we face, it's important—it's imperative that you handle it all your way. We will be anxiously waiting for your next exciting move."

I feel so very close to God tonite that I just can add no more to the love that he has given because, as we discussed tonite by phone, since God is love and our love for each other is all directly from God, then we really have the only true love that exists.

Goodnite to you, God, and to you, Frances, I love you both and it's fabulous!

Charles

* * *

Miami, Florida, December 10th—or is it the 11th—must be the 11th

Dearest Charles:

Just finished talking to you on the phone this morning which I thought was real exciting, and somehow or other, I don't think it was a surprise to you, or at least you sounded like you had just known I was going to call.

Such a love affair. It really strengthens my faith and trust in God, and not only that, it really has created even greater dependence upon Him, because all I can say is I'd never trust myself with the decisions we've been making madly with no discussion or worry—just communication with God and that's all. (THAT'S ALL?) Who needs anything else!

And now you want to know what that laughing picture says that I sent you? What it really says is that I knew the answer before you knew the question, so that must make me pretty smart, or some-

143

thing. All I can say is it's a good thing the Lord will be keeping me busy the last ten days before you get here or I don't think I'd be able to stand it. Isn't He smart because He understands us so well? He arranged for me to do the thing that will really keep me anchored to reality instead of just sailing off into orbit which is what I feel like right now.

Now to answer something you said on the phone last night about your home. There has never been anything ever even flicker across my mind except living there. And I think it's fabulous how the Lord brings each one of these little areas into the open and places them in our minds, not just for consideration, but rather for confirmation. Now I say this, not even knowing what your home looks like or anything else even though you did point it out to me when we went to your church. I don't even remember the color or anything else, never dreaming at that moment of what might possibly happen in the future. As a matter of fact, would you believe I even wrote a book called *God Is Fabulous* before I ever realized the fabulousity of God, because He really is. When you realize what He has done through just a few hours in each other's presence (but definitely all in HIS presence) anyone would have to admit what a fabulous God He is.

I really loved your thoughts on "floating freedom" —and that is really so true. I'm going to have to incorporate a lot of these thoughts in *Hang Loose With Jesus*—but who knows, there might be another book just prior to that one because I feel the next one has to be dedicated to you. And would you believe that I've known for quite some time now that the next one had to be dedicated to you regardless of what it was about. And see how the Lord kept down any jealousy in my family, because Book No. 1 was dedicated to the "men" in my life. Book No. 2 to Joan, and Book No. 3 to Tom. See how the Lord took care of all problems?

My own life is UNREAL, Charles, because God solved every problem area. Probably one of the biggest stumbling blocks would have been my home and yet I just up and sold it because I knew it was what the Lord wanted even though I didn't know why. And for me this was something, because I'm the kind who puts her roots down deep because when I love, I love FOREVER, and I really loved my home, but I have never had one minute's regret and have never been able to understand it except that I knew beyond a shadow of a doubt that God had spoken.

Oops, my luv, just looked at my watch and realized that I have to get to work, so I'll just send this one off real quick and when I have time I'll scribble you a few more lines.

Charles, I can't wait to see what the Lord is going to do with our lives. Somehow or other, I have the definite feeling it will be to communicate love—but not the usual kind but a very special love because it's of God. Did it ever dawn on you what this could do to the lives of young people to discover that age is no barrier to exciting love when God is behind it all.

I LOVE YOU, I LOVE YOU, I LOVE YOU, I LOVE YOU, I LOVE YOU, I LOVE YOU, I LOVE YOU.

. . . and all because of Him,
Frances

* * *

Miami, Florida
December 12, 1969

Dearest Charles:

Just hung up the telephone and even though we closed in prayer, I still had to send an extra little prayer up to God, thanking him for calling me to be the missing ingredient in your life, and thanking him for never revealing to me that anything at all was missing in my life until He decided himself to give me the superabundant life He so generously offers.

And are you aware of the fact that both of us have a tremendous desire to GIVE instead of take. I am only concerned with how much love, devotion, joy and excitement I can put into your life. And I'm so well aware of the fact that your only desire is to *give* of the love that God has given to you for me. You may not even be aware of how great is your desire to give of everything you have to bring additional happiness into my life, but in every sentence you say, that desire comes out.

And I was so delighted to hear you say on the phone this morning that you didn't believe that God would ever allow us to have an argument. You know, Charles, there are people who will disagree with you violently on this subject, but I happen to feel exactly the same way that you do. I've even heard people say your life would have to be extremely dull without a disagreement or fight, or whatever you want to call it, but I can't think of anything more exciting than never having to get mad at you. SO THERE!

All I can think of right now is "My cup runneth over!" because my cup of happiness, joy and peace is absolutely running over, even though the peace right now is a real exciting, turbulent peace (if there is such a thing), but I'm sure you know exactly what I mean. When God does things, He really does them up right.

I'm exhausted, so I'm going to sneak into bed right now and see if I can't get rid of the bags under my eyes, but I wanted to put this piece of paper in the typewriter so that I could fall right out of bed in the morning and write you a few more dreams. Nope, can't do that, because I never dream because life in Christ is so real, there's no need to dream for more exciting things, because He really gives them to us. All I can say is P.T.L.

How 'bout that? Here it is morning and I still feel the same as I did last night. First thing I did when I woke up this morning (and I really *slept* last night) was to reach over for your picture to see if I honestly believed you were real. Now I'm going over and dial your number and wake you up. So there!

Mission accomplished! And here I go again on a cloud for today as well. No more for now, because I've got to get to the bank today, to the Christian Women's Club, get a lot of work done at the office and then to Lake Worth tonight. And when I finally get all that done, then I'll get to talk to you.

In His fabulosity,

Frances

* * *

Houston, Texas, Saturday 5:30 P.M.
December 13, 1969

Dearest Sweetheart,

I'm lonesome! For a moment (a very long one) I feel you have been taken away from me—no call tonite.— (Even exclamation marks don't know what to do.) But, you know what? It's for Jesus Christ so all is completely agreeable with me and this is probably something which will be a part of our lives—you going away from home (our home) on speaking engagements for God and with his perfect plan being carried out in our lives, he will make it all just fabulous. Guess I should tell you I had a minute of one of my Holy Spirit weeping spells today about you dashing off for ten days for something great for God and this wasn't from being lonesome, it was sheer Godly joy and thankfulness that for no reason except God and Christ Jesus (what other reason is there?) you venture out on these fantastically busy trips, just loving God and having no other wish in your heart. I love you for it!

And speaking of love—I LOVE YOU!! and love you, and love you, and love you. Mmmmmmmmmm!

Tonite as I reached for a new sheet of paper and my arm went around your picture and pitter pat, pitter pat!! You had better tape your ribs on December 23rd because I expect to squeeze you with all the TNT of love I have for you. Just saw an underlined scripture in Phillips translation (2 Cor. 5:11 plus): "All this is God's doing, for he has reconciled us to himself through Jesus Christ." I'd love to meet you in person sometime, stranger, but I know now all I'll ever need to know about you is the love of God in you. Since all the love that we know for each other came through Christ, it's genuinely pure love! This must have been the way Adam and Eve first felt before they sinned. He will always be our "filter" because we will always receive our love through Him. And you express it so well—"Who needs anything else!" When you said in your letter I received about an hour ago "Such a love affair . . . I'd never trust myself with the decisions we've been making madly with no discussion or worry" I thought about my conversation with a friend and his wife as she seemed to be eagerly gasping for a breath of the excitement I have for God. I said I had tossed one of the biggest events of my life to God and asked him to make all decisions and that I am calmly aware that he will do it in a perfect way. I promised to tell them the question and answer when God had completed his action! I wonder when God will send out wedding announcements!!! And He will too, very soon I hope.

This morning my three letters (two to England and one to North Carolina) were air mailed with my article "thing" and *God Is Fabulous* and *Go, Man, Go* enclosed, and with a prayer that the contents of the envelope would work marvels for God in England. By tomorrow "you" should be in England (probably already have been there many times in your books).

Your comments about having no thoughts except to make this house "our" home came with such complete acceptance on your part that God must have given you another answer fast and sure. It is completely up to God and you. Maybe in early February we can get new furnishings selected for part of the home. Wish we knew God's plans, but this will really be exciting. He probably already has the furniture ordered. A thought (???) has crossed my mind two or three times. When is Joan's school out in Miami? That's too long!!! When is this semester over???! It's beautiful how you expressed God's constant control when you said "I think it's fabulous how the Lord brings each one of these little areas into the open and places them in our minds, not just for consideration, but rather for confirmation." Yes, He really is fabulous!!

You must have also received one of his "confirmations" in the inspiration of the magnitude of communicating love unbound by age to young people. It must have been a thrill to see this kind of love transmitted by Pat Boone and his wife. This we have as a marvelous assurance by the actions of God already in bringing us together, that when He says he will give blessings and joy beyond anything we can imagine or dream, we had better be prepared for a tremendously happy and thrilling and unusual life together. WOW! And He will do it too, just because we gave ourselves to him completely. This is the Kingdom of God on earth! And we are moving into the finest quarters of his mansion!

As my love flows continuously to you in rapidly increasing waves, this letter will continue until the minute I find the address to which it will be mailed. I love you, Frances! Oooooooo!

7:20 Saturday nite. Of course I'm tingling after just

receiving your call from Atlanta. It was quite a thrill to hear the phone ring *instantly* as I closed the first installment of this letter. You just don't know how thrilled I was to hear your voice. Except Monday nite at the Mission Home Station and Wednesday nite choir, I'll remain close to the phone.

You said suddenly you knew just the thing for my Christmas present. Back to your letter—"He confirmed" what would be very meaningful by placing the thought in your mind. I'm sure it will be just great—a piece of ribbon to wrap around you and a tag saying, "To Charles, I love you!" That's all I want. It's double thrilling how He told you; and on December 2 he picked your gift. It's a wonder He didn't just bring them to us without even letting us know. He is really a great God!

I just looked again and again and again and again at the last paragraph of your letter—TWO LINES OF I LOVE YOU. You should feel my heart as I read both lines at once and felt your love flow in twice as fast!!

9:00 P.M. Sunday (10:00 your time). Bang, Bang, Bang, Bang!!! Don't think I could have made it without your call. They can spare you three minutes? I loved your call and love you. 10:30 P.M. I finished all the cards and notes I had been working on so I can mail them tomorrow morning.

SPECIAL DELIVERY - SPECIAL PICTURE - I LIKE!!

Now I have a picture for my wallet. You might be interested that I took Jeanne's picture out as I put yours in. OK? I love you, you know. Until I read your letter today I didn't realize the extent of our both wanting to give and it is really true, because everything you have written and spoken has been very *outgoing*. I'll try to keep you from ever having an occasion to get mad at me, so there, right back!

I liked (loved) your picture, so who knows, maybe I'll recognize you in Miami! The more I look at both your pictures the more deeply I love you. One week plus one day!

Not many lovers can describe their "running over" happiness as a real exciting, turbulent peace, but what else!? I wonder if we will ever stop talking when we are together *next* week.

I would love to be with you as you dash madly through five plus talks a day—radio, TV and probably other media as you transmit God's love so strong that lives bow to Christ in vast numbers. It would still be worth it if only one per week or per month would find a fertile, rich soil and become a burning bush for Christ. I'm awed at the magnitude of your work for Christ! This is a miracle in itself—that you give your all for Christ in such an enthusiastic splendor that the angels in Heaven don't get enough sleep trying to keep their rejoicing updated, because when one is won to Christ they rejoice. Keep 'em busy, gal!!

Don't know how you find time to reread letters, but I'll guarantee if I didn't get one any day I would be reading back-dated ones. I usually have the last two or three out where I've been through them at least three or four times. The sweetness keeps getting sweeter each time I read one, and each new one is even sweeter. Well, after all, it should be because we have already been in love and admitted it for over a week!! God is fabulous and I love the speed he uses!

The more I look at your two pictures the prettier you get and you look like in today's picture you are about to explode with joy and your other picture looks like you just did! What a beautiful radiance of happiness and you didn't know what else God had in store for us when those were made.

Maybe Thursday nite I'll get to read *Hot Line to Heaven* again. Get all these cards and letters for Christmas on their way, and then I'll settle down to things I like better.

I had better close this letter because it will take a whole day for you to read it.

Goodnite sweet,
Charles

* * *

Alabama, Monday Afternoon 12/15/69

Dearest Charles:

By the time you receive this, you'll probably know

the Lord did it again! Things really seem to happen when I'm on TV. It was just unreal how the Lord prepared hearts. Many people have called concerning the *hunger* and I do mean HUNGER in the M.C.'s heart.

The pastor and I prayed outside the TV station claiming the soul of someone in the TV station. The devil carried off the M.C. to a sales meeting, but before leaving he pleaded with me, "Don't go—please stay and talk with my wife." I did, and I wouldn't have even had to read the Four Spiritual Laws to her. Actually I read portions only—and she prayed to receive Christ and said she was going to convert her husband before the day was over. Before the M.C. left I asked him if I could pray with him. So I claimed his soul with him listening today—my heart was pounding *almost* (not quite) as loud as when I'm talking to you!

Even though I'm seeing miracle after miracle happen, I think it's so exciting to know the Lord intends for us to *share the miracles of life together.* I'm living from miracle to miracle because if I thought of how long, and yet how short it is until I see you, I couldn't stand it. Last nite as I told them in church that God would never call you to do anything he didn't give you a desire for I almost laughed out loud *because of the desire He has placed in my heart for you.* And so you see, I would have liked to have said, "My own life is proof!"

Now it's Monday nite—and the things that happen between the pieces of a letter I write to you!! I had dinner (a very exciting one) with a fabulous family

—and extra guests—I wish you could have been there with me—but then I wish you could be every place with me! It's absolutely unbelievable how I want to share everything with you.

The church service tonight was great. And if I don't get you on the phone tonight—and I'll be crushed if I don't—I'll really have to sleep triple time because I have to leave at 3:30 in the morning for Birmingham, two TV shows and then back again. I have a feeling I'm going to really have to call on the Lord for extra strength tomorrow!

Tuesday A.M. They left me on the TV show for one hour. P.T.L.

No more time—want to mail this. More later. Love you, love you, love you, love you, love you, love you! So there!

Can't wait for 4:30 Tuesday!

Love you!
Frances

*   *   *

Houston, Texas
Monday 10 P.M.
December 15, 1969
"Hurry time"

My dearest Sweetheart,

God is fabulous—WOW! What a great nite. Back to the Mission Home. About 12-14 people, God and the devil were present and yes, God really is Fabulous! A mother with three girls (teens) were there. The husband had died just a day or two or few ago (they didn't give any details and I knew nothing

155

about it till after dismissal). They said she was completely sealed off from any talking and the girls probably didn't know how to respond, but the lady started talking freely after my witnessing and those in the mission were excited about this. There was another young, nice-looking lady in her early 20's, if that old, and had been a Christian only one and a half weeks. She had several questions and the Holy Spirit was melting her heart. Another woman kept popping into the spirit of the communion with comments that only tore away, but God's power, as always, is abundantly sufficient. I know what you mean now—you have experienced just this (did you tell me or is it in a book of yours?). With you having such a tremendous experience every day for hours I don't know how you can contain the thrills of it—tonite was really great. Maybe we can develop a stereo talk-recorder so we can make one record and both talk at once—maybe we could catch up on our talking by 1999 or 2099!

I came rushing home at 10:00 and the phone rang and I grabbed it and it was not you._(sad mark). I'm sitting by the phone hoping you will get at least a short minute to call, but if you don't, I'll know God is using you in the exciting way I asked him. I prayed that this would be the most fabulous week of your life.

One week from tomorrow and you will for the first time be in my arms and I can hardly wait! I really love you and it grows stronger every day—it's going to be a very powerful love by 4:30 next Tuesday! The "too happy" expression in the picture which was taken with the now missing person was only that happy because of God and you.* I had to just about bite my tongue that evening to not spend the whole evening talking about you, which I probably only mentioned once or twice—in each sentence.

Christmas lights and decorations are beginning to look beautiful in our neighborhood. Wish you were here to enjoy them with me. I hope you and Joanie will both love the home and I feel you will—but if at any time you feel otherwise we will move post haste. It will be fun planning.

I've been thinking of Tom, but to pray more than "Thanks, Lord God" seems unnecessary, because our hands must remain opened with palms down so we don't try to take it away from God. He is doing and will continue to do his usual marvelous job without our help—only in our release to him.

I can just feel the enthusiasm in your voice and actions as you relentlessly open your life this week for God. I'm anxious to have you tell me lots of exciting details in Miami! Wish I could have seen your TV show.

I love you, I love you, I love you, I love you, I love you, I love you. Hope you are not disappointed— well, because I TRUST God for this being his doing, I know everything will be perfect—even your love in accepting my faults, because with the exchange of

*Charles had enclosed a picture taken while dining out with Molly. It was interesting what he had done with the picture! He had sliced it right down between the two of them, moved Molly's picture over to the side and in between had made a heart and printed the initials FEG in the middle of it! My daughter immediately removed Molly's picture, inserted a picture of me, xeroxed a copy of the entire thing and returned it to Charles telling him it looked better the new way!

our mutual capacity to love each other, faults will probably never be noticed. Too bad I'm so humble I can't think of any of them to tell you!

11:30. The phone just rang and it didn't come through again. It just MUST ring again right away. Please, please, please.

Thank you God, it did, it did!! You sure know how to excite me—can't wait—see you in Birmingham next plane!! Better not. For real—my heart is just thumping. Hope you can get right to sleep and again tomorrow afternoon, too. Please take good care of you for me—after all you are my 1969 Christmas present which will last all our lives together.

Goodnight with a glowing love,

♡ WOW ♡

Charles

It was beautiful the way you are already letting this new found love go into others! Wait till we can do it together!

* * *

Alabama, December 15, 1969

Charles, dear,

I have a feeling I write better when I'm not lying down, but it's after midnight and I just bathed and flopped into bed.

I have a real sneaky feeling this is going to be an exciting church just from talking to the pastor and his wife. We've had about four prayer circles and I just got here at 9 o'clock! I've got your picture on the bed here so I can keep my eye on you while I'm writing.

Wasn't that a real extra blessing the Lord gave us

158

in letting you be there when I called from Atlanta. Somehow or other I know He'll allow us to share our excitement and love during this coming week.

Do you feel as I do that I'm watching all of this take place? But I'm really enjoying what God is doing! A fantastic thought just struck me. I wonder if you would have even asked me out if we were not both Christians? I doubt it! Now that I think about it, have you asked me out yet? Would you even believe our love affair if you weren't a Christian? You'd probably think we both belonged in a NUT HOUSE if you didn't understand how God works.

Talk about spiritual goosepimples—I think just for a moment and a brief one at that, God gave me a preview of heaven because I suddenly discovered my heart pounding away!

No more tonight—more in the A.M. LOVE YOU, LOVE YOU, LOVE YOU, LOVE YOU!

Goodnight, m'luv!
FRANCES

Sunday nite (same letter)

Charles, dear—

I was miserable after I talked to you tonight because it was for such a short time. It seemed just awful that I had to run so fast when I wanted to just have your arms wrapped around me over the telephone wires. Honestly, I was so excited when I saw the opportunity to have you even if it was just for a moment—my heart just sang when you answered the phone.

When I think of how God plants the desires in our

hearts for the things he has for us, it's unreal. Just think how He causes our hearts to quicken just in saying hello over a skinny little wire! I'm looking at your picture and was thinking tonight as I was conducting the soul-winners class and talking about total surrender and telling them how I KNOW God will never let you down if you trust and obey. I can only think of our mutual trust in God. If I didn't really believe what I share I would run so fast right now. Common sense tells me things like this just don't happen. They don't work. It's impossible, and yet I was never more certain of anything in my entire life than I am of God's hand in our relationship. While I was listening to the little kids sing Christmas carols tonight, I was reminded of the faith of a little child—just believing God; it was magnificent how God revealed why I had no choice really but to fall in love with you. I won't try to explain in a letter—I'll wait until I see you. So instead of using common sense I'm exercising Faith. And I'll be running— straight into your arms next Tuesday.

This must be CPA year because I had lunch with a CPA and his family today. I hope you appreciate the great hardship you're putting me through! *I want to tell the whole world about what God has given me—I want them all to know about you!* But I'm being a real good girl and drooling over you in private.

This is an exciting church here. P.T.L. The response has been fabulous! This was one of those congregations and pastor who loved me before I even got here! And it's so much easier this way. And it's so much more exciting.

Charles, I just can't believe—15, (after midnight) 16, 17, 18, 19, 20, 21, 22—and then YOU! God is so fabulous to have had such perfect timing. I don't believe I could have waited six months to see you again.

Will be looking for letters and secret telephone so I can talk to you. But most of all, I'll be looking for you. I don't know how it's possible. I only know it's true.

I LOVE YOU!
and all because of Him,
Your
Frances

*   *   *

Alabama—Tuesday evening, December 16, 1969

Charles, darling:

Just finished talking to you—and how wonderful it is to know that God gave us a few real private moments to share with each other.

When I think about all that has happened in our love affair through Christ in our letters, I can only say *"Nothing* is impossible to God!" I can't believe this. It doesn't make human sense, but God knows and I almost cracked up after I told you what Joan said. This is something we'll really pray about because I'm like you—I don't believe all this—I'm just waiting on God. There are problems, especially with my bookings. And even though the Lord knows, you might not know—the lease on my apartment expires March 13.

Let's pray, m'luv—knowing God will give us the right answer in all things. And somehow trusting in

Him makes all the decisions so easy. As I have thought about all this, do you realize what God's perfect timing is? I built a wall of Jericho around my heart many years ago—and only when I released Tom completely was *I* released to fall in love. And I met you one week later, and the walls of Jericho started tumbling down.

Lost two of my good pens on this trip so bought some cheap ones today—lost a Parker and a Cross—so I bought red ink for the blood of Christ—and for LOVE! TV was great today—I'll just have to share all this in person, but we'll have so much to say and *do* when you get to Miami!

To bed, my love—even with a nap I need sleep. I love you beyond belief, because with my heart and soul I believe God did it all!

I feel like I'm going to explode because my heart is so full of love.

Because I love you,
Frances

* * *

Houston, Texas
December 17, 1969 10:15 P.M.
     18
      19
       20
        21
         22
          23

My dearest you!!
I LOVE YOU. . . .
Not only have I been thinking of you all day, but also talking about you.

Wonder what fabulous things God has been doing with my Frances today. Working you very hard I'm sure but when you know it's for God you are so completely willing you wouldn't want it any other way. Received your first hand-written letter of this trip written Saturday and Sunday. Just in case you don't know it, I love you for taking time to write when you have worked two days every day. Of course, I might just die if I didn't get the letters regularly.

Had a wonderful day going to and from Lake Charles and so far as I could tell God had several people prepared to hear what he said through me. Christmas caused a small attendance of about fifty-four. I had asked God to make me the calmest I had ever been in a talk and He really did. Also he furnished all the words, as always. They want another day so I may return again.

I brought the soloist back to Houston. She's getting married December 28th. I made a comment about what a marvelous witness they could be by having Christ's love and their love reflected in their lives. I told her about Pat and Shirley Boone and so pray that they will be inspired to do the same.

I guess this had better be the last letter I mail to Clyde's address—rest will be to Miami and I may be there first! Maybe I can have a short one when you get home. You won't have time to rest if I make it long.

God's sense is far more sensible than common which (common sense) neither of us have considered using—the devil suggested it to both of us but I'm glad he was chased off. I wonder how God will use us as a team! He will really know how and it will probably be totally unlike anything we could concoct. This crossed my mind as I was going to Lake Charles while you are working away in Alabama. It's just before midnite there and I keep hoping for a call, but maybe we could live a day without one but I can't think of anything worse!

No, I really wouldn't believe our love affair except for our mutual trust in God which caused Him to plan our lives. Since I love you so much now, I could now fall in love with you, but it wouldn't be a perfect love and all my letters would just be "Dear Mrs. Gardner, How are you, I'm just fine, Yours truly."

TELEPHONE!

You just don't know how beautiful your prayer was tonite and your talk about family love. You'd better be careful or you'll have everyone in the U.S. loving the right way before we can show them! I think it was marvelous that you asked couples to dedicate their love for Christ and for each other at the altar today. I have a feeling this is the beginning of the greatest love affair that ever happened to Christians. I hope God will cause this to spread like wildfire! And you and I can fan the fire!! I think it is utterly fabulous that God had us both telling the same thing today and even to using the 13th chapter of 1st Corinthians. Did you say "Hot Line to Heaven"? With this consistency with which God always answers prayers from us about the mission we have, why shouldn't we "toss" our lives to him and just say, "Catch them, Lord God, and use them like you want them" because even on top of the thrill that comes when we feel his positive answer, we are

164

given so much for ourselves just because He is a Great God. I love you!

Here's a real sweet goodnite kiss for you—Miss Teen-ager—since you feel "15" which, incidentally, makes you younger than Joan. I'm honored that Joan looked to me for an answer she needed and I love her for it.

How sweet it is!! I love you with all my heart.

Charles

* * *

Houston, Texas, December 17, 1969
17-18-19-20-21-22-23
hurry hurry hurry
        Don't hurry any more

Dearest Sweetheart,
I like that!

How's my TV Girl tonite? How many directors, weather girls, cameramen, etc. accepted Christ to-day—after all—two programs. And you will never know the tremendous effect it will have and has had on the TV audience. It's refreshing and people are very thirsty!

I hope you had a chance for a nap knap napp. I hope you got a bit o'sleep this afternoon. I would be concerned about you but I know you are doing every second of your work for God, so why have any concern that he will take care of you. That doesn't mean that he doesn't expect you to rest when you get a chance. What an abundant life you have and how marvelous that God gives you these fabulous experiences.

Speaking of fabulous—a wealthy Christian client

of mine called today and AB (after business) he said, "How are you doing?" and quickly and enthusiastically I said, "Fantastic!" He said, "Isn't that someone else's word?" And I said, "No, that is FABULOUS!" He said let's get together for lunch so you can tell me some of the excitement. He never has fully felt the excitement I have—but anyway he recognizes I'm excited about God in a way he wants to hear more about.

I think about what you are doing constantly and know you are having a really fabulous trip. I went to a meeting tonite with some businessmen about a safety device for autos, and as "sales excitement about making money, etc." goes I guess they get excited, but I wouldn't trade my two hours last nite at the mission for all the money in the world. As much as I love my work, it isn't nearly as interesting as when you have just seen a life won for Christ or someone suddenly find God is very real.

Saw a client of mine in the hall today—she is one who is one of the outstanding businesswomen in Texas, and God opened up for about five minutes and she loves excitement so she said, "You make all the things I do sound so mundane." (How true she spoke.) I said, "With your marvelous personality and reputation, if you could find this trust in God to combine with it, it would be fantastic!" She again said, "My product just isn't as good as yours." Her product is money—ours is Christ and God! Together let's move her into total surrender for God!

I talked to a friend of mine whose wife is plagued with spinal deterioration which looks from the medical view, to be fatal. He said in regard to our prior talk that he hasn't been able to fully release her in total surrender to God for Him to do her healing His way. I felt a nudge to have him read the article of our experiences and if he then felt he should, his wife could read it. God will use it because I felt God said, "Give it to him." Maybe you can pray with them while you are here. When I told him God promises he will return one hundred times what he accepts when we give, and that I knew how abundantly He gave to me, he said, "Yes, I know because I can see what He has done in your life." I told him that God can make him a powerful Christian as he faces this in total surrender to God. I don't doubt an instant that God can and possibly will choose to heal her physically, but if both of them are healed spiritually then it's worth the cost. I believe also that when they reach total surrender of themselves, then God has the freedom to heal physically, but total surrender doesn't come on a bargaining basis in exchange for healing or anything else.

Clock just struck 11:00 (midnight there) and I keep hoping the phone will ring, although I know how difficult it is for you. I'm kinda selfish when it comes to loving you. I'll just hold some extra space to write a note after you phone. I'll mail this to Clyde's home unless I hear differently.

I called June tonite (before 10:00) and she is doing fine with the Lord, but I don't believe I've ever known of the devil fighting anyone so hard. God must have something great in store for her. Their company is having a party Thursday and apparently they are pretty rough and lots of drinking. One of her bosses told her he was a little disappointed that she had found this total thing (surrender) and wouldn't be drinking and having a good time. She said, "Just watch me have a good time!"

TELEPHONE!!

I love you, I really do, I do, I do, I do. My heart quivers when I talk to you, and tonite was so wonderful!

Next to you loving me, most of all I thank God that He is so absolutely abundant in everything—your fabulous week for Him, the nice room and private bath and private phone and private love.

Goodnite Sweet one, my love for you gets stronger every day and I long to be with you, and it is just around the corner.

I love you,
Charles

*   *   *

Alabama—December 18, 1969—Thursday afternoon.

Charles, my love:

I'm GLAD you're not here. You'd never believe this! I'm sitting on the arm of a big old chair writing on a linoleum-covered, cigarette-burned dresser top. This motel is the absolute end! There is one dim lamp—the bath is *unreal!* You almost have to stand in the toilet to get to the wash basin and mirror. I wouldn't even put my dog in the shower! There is no closet—what a dump! No phone either—and there's no place I can walk to phone you. I walked out to the street and I can't even see a place I can phone from. I'll call you from somewhere tonight—probably from the church. All I can say is P.T.L.A. It's a good thing that I know that God loves me and a great big special thank you to Him for letting you love me. Between your love and His I'll make it through the night!

Darling, if I didn't have your letters to hang on to I'd walk to Miami right now! Well, praise the Lord anyway, I'm sure a real miracle will come from this!

The pastor who brought me to this town was very antagonistic about the Four Spiritual Laws when I met him Sunday, and today while he was waiting for someone to bring me to his house he led his mailman to the Lord. No longer does he doubt the power of God's Holy Spirit. Honestly, Charles, do you realize that many ministers do not understand the working of the Holy Spirit? No wonder so many churches stay small—they try humanly to build a church.

Did I ever tell you I think you're so clever? Some of the little things in your letter just crack me up! Like the "sad mark".

I was rereading your special delivery No. 2 letter I got this morning and was reading your comments on the pictures I sent you. I'm sure you know I have pictures taken all the time—seems like people have an overabundance of film or something. But those were taken right after I met you. They took six—and I asked if they would mind letting me have three. I wonder if you have any idea as to why I asked for the pictures? And does that tell you why I was looking so happy? I brought them home and stuck them in my desk until the Lord said, "Send them to the guy you had them taken for." Would you believe that's the ONLY time I ever asked for copies of pictures that had been taken?

I think it's so fabulous how God puts thoughts into our heads simultaneously. If you recall, last night I prayed and asked God to let me be the woman you wanted for your own and to not let you see my flaws and defects other than through His eyes—and your letter said exactly the same thing. Isn't it unbelievable how He does this so many times?

I've got to get ready, someone is picking me up shortly. LOVE YOU, LOVE YOU, LOVE YOU, more than you realize.

Because He planned it!

Your

Frances

*   *   *

AUTHOR'S NOTE: On December 13th I left for my last trip of 1969. By this time there was no doubt in either Charles' mind or mine that God had brought us together for a very special reason—and that reason was the uniting of two people to make them one in Christ—in other words MARRIAGE! The "when" was the big question because of my tightly booked schedule, but God took care of this situation beautifully while I was on this trip. Little did I realize when I left for Alabama what would happen before I returned to Miami for the Christmas holidays "to get acquainted with Charles."

I had gone through approximately half of my trip when my daughter called me in Huntsville, Alabama to tell me that my beloved mother-in-law had passed away. She had broken her hip three months earlier and had been hospitalized ever since. My first comment was, "Praise the Lord!" which I sincerely meant with my heart and soul—Praise be to God who let her live long enough for me to share the claims of Christ with her and be there as she accepted Christ as her personal saviour and Lord. There was no doubt in my mind where Grandma would spend eternity.

As I looked upon her last days I remembered the peace with which she accepted the broken hip and she was anxiously looking forward to crossing over into a new world. The last word she had ever said to me was "Amen" as we had formed a living prayer link in the hospital between her bed and another patient in the room. My first thought was to go home to help make funeral arrangements, but then I thought about the people who were waiting to hear what God had to say through me, and I remembered the verse of scripture which says "Let the dead bury the dead," so I continued my tour and on the night of December 18th I went right from the pulpit to the airport and prayed myself right straight through to Miami. At this time of the year the planes are really crowded, but God knew my time was limited, so he saw to it in his magnificent way, that each time I was called as a standby.

By the time I arrived in Miami at 5:00 A.M. I was tired and worn out and had time for a little nap before going to Grandma's funeral. After sleeping for two or three hours, I got up, got out my date books for the next two years and after carefully examining them again, I decided there just simply wasn't any time which would be right to be married, so I sat down at the breakfast table, drank my coffee, and then prayed fervently. I said, "God, I just don't know when Charles and I can get married, but you do, so I'm going to ask you to reveal to me, and confirm to Charles exactly when we should be married!" Then I continued praying about the funeral and for the people attending, etc., and at the end of twenty minutes I finished praying, got up from the table to go into my bedroom, and I had taken about one and a half steps, when God "spoke." (Many people have asked me if God speaks to me in an audible voice saying, "Frances, do this . . ." or "do that. . . ." No, God has never spoken to me audibly yet, but I had an exciting Christian in Ft. Wayne, Indiana, give me her version of God speaking, and I want you to think about this— she said God speaking is "voiceless knowledge!" Think seriously what "voiceless knowledge" means. Isn't that true of how God speaks to us many times?) And so with "voiceless knowledge" which left no doubt it was God speaking, this is what He said: "1969 was Jeanne's, 1970 is yours—start it off right the first minute, at the Party for the Lord." (Remember that Charles' wife Jeanne had died in 1969?)

I was stunned—not because God had answered my prayer so quickly, but because this was exactly eleven days away and Charles didn't even know it yet! However, after all the arguments I had had with God concerning the impossibility of marriage, I wasn't about to argue with him any more, so I accepted this completely improbable date, knowing that I was returning to Alabama this same afternoon

172

and there was no time to plan a wedding or anything else.

As soon as the funeral was over, I was driven back to the airport, and caught a plane to Atlanta, with a prayer that I would catch one to Birmingham in time to make my service in Sylacauga, Alabama that evening. I dropped Charles a little note on the plane in which you will note I asked him to pray fervently asking God to let him know when we should be married, but while I was in Atlanta I decided since the time was so short, I'd better let him know that God had told me when we were to be married, so he could get confirmation of the same date. I had about an hour in Atlanta, so I ran to the telephone and dialed Charles' number praying that he would be home, even though it was earlier than he would normally be home. Somehow or other, Charles "knew" that day to come home early, and he was coming in the front door when the phone rang. There was very little time between planes and I had to get in the standby line, so there was no time to waste. I very simply said to Charles, "Charles, God has revealed to me exactly when we should be married. Now I want you to pray fervently and ask him to confirm it to you." Probably the thing that was the most surprising about our telephone conversation was the complete trust that God would confirm to Charles exactly the same thing he had said to me, and since he happens to be the same kind of a prayer fanatic that I am, there was no doubt whatsoever in his mind that God would let him know the exact time too! He didn't ask me to give him a clue of any kind; his only answer was "OK" and that was all.

God was really watching over me that night, because all the standbys had deposited their tickets with the agent and were waiting to be called. They called six and I was not among them. I sat there praying, knowing this was the only flight I could catch that would put me in Sylacauga in time for my evening service. Soon they began calling the names of the standbys who would not get on the plane. They called out sixty-one names—sixty-one people picked up their tickets, disappointed because they could not get out on the flight, and I was the only one left sitting in this particular section. I walked up to the agent and said, "You didn't call my name either time." He looked straight at me and said, "Are you Frances Gardner?" I said, "Yes." He said, "When you hear the buzzer sound for the closing of the door, pick up your ticket and run for the plane. You're the seventh standby and the last one going on." Then he added, "We didn't call your name, because we didn't want anyone to know that you had gotten the last standby seat." Don't ask me how they knew I HAD to get on that plane, because I don't know. All I do know is that God knew and He arranged it all.

I made it to Sylacauga about twenty minutes late, but the congregation was still singing, and we had a marvelous night for the Lord. When the service was over, I called Charles from the pastor's house, and what a night this was! When Charles answered the phone he said, "I wrote you a letter and I want to read part of it to you!" I thought this was sorta silly because it seemed ridiculous to read it on the telephone if he was going to mail the letter to me, but I said "OK." He didn't say he had prayed, or that God had answered his prayer or anything else, but he read this portion of the following letter to me:

"I feel utterly confident that your answer is also the same exact date and exact time and my heart is about to jump out of my chest!! . . . At the New Year's Eve Party for the Lord at midnight—to start the Fabulous 1970 year."

I ALMOST JERKED THE TELEPHONE RIGHT OFF THE WALL! And yet I don't know why I should have been the least bit surprised because I knew beyond a shadow of a doubt that God would confirm to Charles EXACTLY the same thing he had said to me. And then Charles said a most interesting thing—"By the way, will you marry me?" (You may have noted that Charles had never asked me to marry him. When he got my letter saying "I love you" he had asked me, "When can we get married?") And the scriptures that God had caused me to memorize on November 26, 1969 at 2:00 A.M. were brought to the front of my mind, because it was now God's perfect timing for Charles to hear the answer God had given me for him, and this is what I said (I changed only one word—and that was my name):

"And Frances said, 'Intreat me not to leave thee, or to return from following after thee: for whither thou goest, I will go; and where thou lodgest, I will lodge: thy people shall be my people, and thy God my God: Where thou diest, will I die, and there will I be buried: The Lord do so to me, and more also, if ought but death part thee and me" (Ruth 1:16,17).

I waited breathlessly, feeling that God had an-

swered every problem in our life with these two verses of scripture, but I continued to wait, feeling more romantic and "spiritual" than ever before in my life, but still there was no response from Charles. All of a sudden a real quiet Texas drawl on the other end of the line said, "Yes or no, will you marry me?" I nearly fainted, because the scriptures had answered every question concerning our future lives, and I said, "Charles, didn't you hear the scriptures I just read?" Charles answered in that same soft Texas drawl: "Yes, honey, I heard you say you'd run after me, and that you'd live with me, but honey, I WANT YOU TO MARRY ME!" I assured him the answer was "yes" with no reservations at all! Just another example of God's fabulous sense of humor!

* * *

Miami, Florida, December 19, 1969

Edward, my love.

Nope, don't like that, think I'll make it Charles instead.

I just decided I can't marry you! I bought new luggage after my other stuff got so horribly busted up and it's got the initials FG on it. Now how do you get around that? After all, I can't go running around the country registering under a false name, can I? Isn't that awful. Guess we'll just have to call the whole thing off. But you know what????? I know God's got the answers to every problem, including the answer to the question of what name do all future bookings come out under, etc.

And this morning a bolt of lightning went through me concerning a certain date, and I'll just patiently wait to see if the Lord tells you the same thing (or was this just wishful thinking on my part?). Funny thing, I have thought of all kinds of dates (including the ones that aren't available in my book) but have never had any complete sense of THIS IS IT until something (I wonder what?) put a date into my mind. Well, if the Lord confirms it to you, then I'll know, or I should say, *we'll* know it's right. And peculiarly, I am certain that when the right date is known, God will have transmitted the idea to both of us.

Joan went over to the office and picked up the mail and I got your special delivery letter of a week ago. I shall read it on the plane on the way home. I just read about the first paragraph and can already feel the power of it, and didn't want to read the rest of it until just God and I could share it on the plane on the way back this afternoon.

Loved the letter which accompanied it—but then I love each and every one of your letters. I can't wait until I can hear you say all these things in person. We had a long prayer over breakfast this morning, asking for God's undergirding as we go to Grandma's funeral, and then we really thanked God for giving you to me. All of the verses in the Bible stand behind the one which constantly keeps coming to my mind in relation to you, and that is, "Seek ye *first* the kingdom of God and His righteousness and all these things shall be added to you." And all I can think of is that in putting Christ first you were the extra things He was talking about and a blessing I never even dreamed of. I have said so many, many, many times that I would never even consider getting married again, and boy does our fabulous God make me eat my words over and over. It's a good thing I don't mind spiritual indigestion. But you know really, *I* never did consider getting married. It seemed to me the decision was made by someone else other than me—and not YOU, EITHER!

And now that I think about it, all these plans we're making and thinking about, etc., and you still haven't asked the only question that's important, but again, I think the Lord knows the right timing. I'll really have to restrain myself from giving you the answer before you ask me. And I'm sure you realize by now that the answer is in those two verses of scripture. How God's perfect timing is always the best has really been proven all the way through this entire situation. I'm sure He's going to use all of this in a magnificent way to convince many, many people of the value of listening to God, because His way is always best. I'm sure that *Frances Gardner* would never have spoken to you in Houston if she had even the slightest inkling that first meeting what was going to happen, because as a person I'm sure I would have felt it would have ruined my entire life which was so completely exciting. Only God could have shown me that all He was doing was ADDING to my life, and not taking away. But again, proof that God is so much smarter than we are.

Love you, love you, love you. And this may be the last letter you get from me. I'll try to sandwich in another little note, but whether I do or not, Charles, remember I love you with all my heart, my soul, my body and mind, and excitingly this is possible because in total surrender to God I find great joy in looking to the day when I am united one in Christ with you. Faith, hope and love abide, but the greatest of these is LOVE!

Eternally yours, in the greatest love possible,
Frances

* * *

Friday afternoon en route to Atlanta—12/19/69

To My Beloved:
"O magnify the Lord with me,
And let us exalt His name together!"
This is the verse that really came to my mind today as I thought about the future. And how this verse is so completely in accord with the desires of our hearts—to exalt His name together. I often feel so small in attempting to discover what fabulous things are in store for the future. Somehow I seem to *know* just because God is speaking so plainly right now, what the next step is. PRAY, Charles, as fervently as you have ever prayed—asking God to reveal WHEN! But interestingly enough, this seems to be only the small beginning of what He has in store for us.

I just finished reading "What a Mighty God We Serve" or really "A Tribute to Jeanne," or was it really "A Tribute to God." You see, Charles, you're like I am, once you have emotionally exhausted yourself in writing what God would have you write, the power has gone out of you. I am always drained dry when I finish a book. I feel the reservoir has run dry and in a dry state I can never appreciate what I have written—that is why I feel you cannot appreciate what you wrote as much as I can.

I felt a fantastic love and greeted it with mixed emotions—joy at your ability to love, and concern as to whether or not I could ever deserve the same kind of love. My constant prayer is that God will mold me into the "perfect(?)" woman for you. I don't want to be perfect in anyone's eyes but yours, and only God can do the job, but how fabulous a God we serve who can do just that.

I look to the future with no qualms or reservations—no fear because "perfect love casteth out fear"—no jealousy because jealousy is not of God—but only belief and trust that God has done it all so that we may truly "exalt His name *together*."

My heart ached so for Jan at the funeral today. Tom never put his arm around her once—and horribly enough he didn't even shed one tear. Poor boy—his heart has become so hardened—but when it melts, it will really melt! I only pray that Jan doesn't have a nervous breakdown. How I pray that God will use you to bring this family together.

As we left the funeral parlor today Joan said, "I lost one grandmother—and am gaining one grandmother (your mother)." And then Jan said, "And I've never had a father-in-law (that's YOU, you know)—and now Brant's going to have a grandfather" (that's you, you know). Look what you're going to acquire. How will it feel to become a father, and a grandfather and a father-in-law at the same time!!! (Along with becoming something else too!)

All of us except Tom are anticipating the most glorious Christmas ever and I pray the Lord will surprise even hardhearted Tom.

I do not know how to tell you more than I have

how I love you—it seems I have poured out my very soul in this letter because my heart is overflowing. May you read this in the great love with which I write. Right now I feel the great love of God just pouring out of me like a mighty river and splashing all over you, and completely engulfing you.

Forever—with God,
Frances

*   *   *

Houston, Texas
December 19, 1969
8:30 P.M.—our time

My dearest Sweetheart,

I don't know just how steady my writing will be because God just gave me an answer at 8:20 to a prayer which started when you called from Atlanta about 5:00 this evening. I can't wait for your call to-nite! You said God had given you a clear answer rather suddenly as to the date and time of our marriage, but you would not tell me so God would give me the same answer. WOW! I just didn't know how and when the answer would come, but not only is God Fabulous—he's FAST. And exciting!! I really wasn't quite prepared for the answer he gave, but I am now fifteen minutes after I have had time to regain my composure.

Here's what happened: I was rather tired because last night I reread *Hot Line to Heaven* for the third reading and didn't get to bed till 2:00 o'clock. And just to throw in an extra blessing, reading this fantastic book put me through over two nervous hours of the greatest emotional thrills I have ever known. I cried and laughed and loved Christ, God, you, Joanie, Tom and Jan all the way through it. I think it was real neat for God to do this the nite before he told me our exact date and exact time of the wedding, and I feel utterly confident that your answer is also that same exact date and exact time and my heart is about to jump out of my chest!!

It is also interesting to note that after I talked to you, I read the article about Jeanne's and my experiences and I really feel his reason for that (at least one reason) was to put fresh in my mind the tremendous feeling that thrills your whole body (and I say that literally) when God speaks directly and positively to you. Right now (8:45) my feet, legs, arms and actually my whole body is tingling with more than excitement. After the article I went to bed and slept for about an hour, but after I was in bed I asked God to reveal to me as plain as to you the date he had selected for our wedding. By the way—"WILL YOU MARRY ME?!" Then I slept. When I woke up at 8:20, the feeling came and almost like it did the three times God once said to me, "Charles, let me do this my way!" Tonite he said:

"At the New Year's Eve Party for the Lord at midnite—to start the fabulous 1970 year." We have both known he was planning for us together!!! I just know you received the same time when he told you. I really didn't expect it so soon, but then God has been way ahead of us in every single step in this long courtship (October 3 when we met until today December 19th—77 days—here we are back to God's numbers again). WOW—PTL!! I LOVE YOU!!

TELEPHONE!!! Next to a call from you I would rather have the call I just received than any other in the world because it was from another lady that I love almost as much as I do you—Joanie! We had a great and nice long talk and I'm thrilled. I thought it was real neat (by the way, the phone rang just as I finished writing "I love you!")—real neat when Joanie said she and Tom just never believed you would ever marry again and to see you so excited that you couldn't talk of anything but me; and she had seen you on spiritual cloud 9, but now you are on cloud a million!! She's really interesting to talk to and puts excitement into her thoughts so cleverly expressed. Isn't it great that she called so we could get to know each other better. I loved her Special Delivery letter today and felt it packed with her love.

I was just recalling something interesting about the way the Holy Spirit talked to me at 8:20. Just as I was waking up my mind seemed flooded with an unusual feeling and then this clear message came kind of in the region back of my forehead in the front center of my brain area, not like a normal thought—it is a powerful, strong feeling of God's presence in my mind—that must be at least partly what he means by "Father, as I am in you and you in me" and then as he is in us. That is really awesome! Thanks to God for this.

Same letter—continued Saturday 12:15 A.M. (12/20/69)

183

As I was reading and reading and reading Ruth 1:16, 17 I realized the blessing of God speaking so vividly to me—He would not do less for you than the miracles and his speaking to me in March; the same God who takes away when we are his disciples assures us he will give in return everything better for his purpose and give it abundantly more than we can ever dream or imagine. Frances, God is so fabulous! Do you think we can take all he will give? This is for sure that you and I will give to him everything of our lives and will be available to him without consideration of our personal desires, but you just can't give to God as fast or as much as he gives us. And it all depends on one simple thing—to wrecklessly *(note spelling)* TRUST God and only ask for what we know for sure to be for fulfilling his purpose.

How beautifully he put it before you that 1969 was for Jeanne and 1970 for you. 1970 from the first minute will all be for you under the full direction of God personally.

Now let me copy I Corinthians 12:27-31 from the Phillips translation. Of course, you instantly named the greatest gift—LOVE. We were in thanks to God for personally talking to us both today, you at 10:30 this morning (12/19) and me at 8:20 P.M., talking about how God must have gone into the very best part of heaven's treasury vault, looked at his supply of gifts and picked the very best for us, and this is what he has given us:

"Now you are together the body of Christ, and individually you are members of him. And in his Church God has appointed FIRST some to be his

MESSENGERS. . . . You should set your hearts on the best spiritual gifts, but I shall show you a way which surpasses them all"—Christian Love! Your burning, exciting desire for the love between us through Christ and God to be a powerful witness to other couples to let their love be demonstrated to others is tremendously fabulous and we know God will do just that. How thankful we are!

With utter assurance that God had given you the same answer as he had given me (because his talking to me tonite was no ordinary thing) it was tremendously awesome when you answered what God said to you at 10:30 A.M. after I read the first part of my letter to you; that from the first instant of 1970 our wedding would start, and you said it came to you like a bolt of lightning struck. For God to do this real neat display of his love for us is so marvelous and thrilling that even now at about 1:00 o'clock A.M. I'm still unable to feel a real part of this world. Thank you our God for completely arranging everything for us and we haven't disorganized your plan because we are anxious to *wrecklessly* (note spelling again) toss the rest of our lives to you and really not care how you use them—we trust you, Lord God, and how marvelous you have been to us. Thank you with all our hearts. Amen!

With abundant love,
Charles
(see you Tuesday 4:30)

* * *

This is the last letter written before our marriage.

Houston, Texas 11:55 P.M.-Sat.
December 20, 1969

Hi, you sweet bundle of love:

Just finished another most wonderful telephone "love date" with the most wonderful person in all the world, and oh, how I love you! You do know you are in for a tremendous love because not only do you get all the love I'm capable of giving, but I asked God on 12/20 to let me love you beyond anything I had ever known—and He did!*

It is just now "instantly after midnite" and my heart jumped to realize that in exactly eleven days you will be one with me!" "God giveth us richly all things to enjoy." And He is giving me the very best in his kingdom and I'm most grateful and aware of this—it really humbles me.

*Charles and Jeanne had a beautiful marriage and his love for her was so intense it kept him from putting God first in his life for many years, and it was only as he released her and put God first did Christ really transform Charles' life. Because of this great love for her, he didn't ever want it to stand in the way of our love, and for this reason he asked for a love "beyond anything I have ever known." No lack of respect for her whatsoever, but a desire to have OUR marriage perfect.

186

This letter is short, but it carries to you all of my love and God's love!

Goodnight, sweetheart,
Charles

I LOVE YOU

*   *   *

AUTHOR'S NOTE: Now please don't feel that all of our excitement ended just because God had told us when we were to get married. Wait until you see what happened next. . . . I returned to Miami on December 22nd, and Charles arrived on the 23rd. There had been a very interesting problem of whether or not we would recognize each other because of only having seen each other for such a short time in Houston three months prior to this, although there was no doubt in either of our minds as to what God wanted out of our lives. As I was getting dressed to go to the airport to meet Charles I remembered that he had said he wanted me wrapped up with a big bow and a tag saying, "Charles, I love you!"; so my daughter-in-law printed a regular Christmas tag saying, "For Charles—from God"—and then she made the comment, "If God didn't give you to Charles, then nobody did!" And I turned the card over on the reverse side and wrote: "I love you" and signed it simply "Frances."

By this time I was beginning to have butterflies in my stomach because I was wondering how I should greet Charles. After all, since I had never had a date with him, I certainly wasn't going to kiss him, so I thought the proper thing to do would be to shake hands with him, but then I decided that was a little too formal since we were getting married in just a few days. Just as I started out the door of my apartment I saw a little cardboard sign which was taped above the light switch. It said, "Lord, what wilt thou have me to do?" I tore it off the wall, grabbed a pin, and pinned it on my suit, and this is exactly how I went to the airport . . . with a Christmas tag and a big red bow pinned in my hair, and a tag on the front of my suit saying, "Lord, what wilt thou have me to do?"

After all my teasing of Charles telling him that if he was coming in at 4:30, I was leaving on the four twenty-nine, we were delayed by an unusual amount of traffic, and didn't arrive in time. His plane had come in, and I raced down the concourse to the gate where his plane had come in, and NO CHARLES! I ran down to the luggage carousels, and he wasn't there. My daughter, daughter-in-law and grandson were waiting on the lower level and I asked them if they had seen anyone who looked like Charles, but they hadn't, so I flew back upstairs again. I didn't see him anyplace, so I ran to the paging counter and was waiting in line to have him paged when all of a sudden my heart skipped a beat, because standing there was my beloved, and there was no doubt in my mind who he was. I was riveted to the spot where I stood as God's love poured all over me.

Charles saw me the same instant I saw him and he set a new track record for the airport terminal. I can only say that apparently God had spoken to him about what to do when he met me, because there was no indecision in his mind as to what to do. He had seen the sign "Lord, what wilt thou have me to do?"

. . . and he did it! He kissed me tenderly, beautifully and with his arms tightly pressed around me we both felt completely bathed in God's wonderful love. I'm sure that somewhere in that embrace a mutual prayer went up to God because two people had exactly the same thought: "Thank you, Lord!"

We left the upper terminal and went downstairs for Charles to meet his new daughter and his daughter-in-law and grandson. Charles had no children by his previous marriage, so he acquired a lot of things in this union.

We went to church that night to see the Living Nativity, and Charles met my pastor, and some members of the church, most of whom were shocked beyond belief because they hadn't even known that I was corresponding with anyone, let alone falling in love or thinking about marriage. The next day we called about going down to get our marriage license and discovered to our dismay that all the county offices in Dade County, Florida were closed for one week to give all the employees an opportunity for a holiday vacation. I urgently called my physician who made arrangements for us to have our blood tests done in the emergency ward of the hospital, which we immediately did, and then we waited until Monday, December 29th to go down to the county clerk's office to apply for our marriage license.

What happened then was like a three ring circus. We applied on Monday, and were told to return on Wednesday to pick up the license since we were being married Wednesday night (actually Thursday morning since God had said the first minute of

1970), so we flew back to my apartment and began the mad business of packing my things to go to Houston, since we knew we had to get to our new home in Houston quickly, because seven days after we were married I had to leave for my first tour. Charles had asked me if I wanted to go to the Bahamas for our honeymoon when he first got to Miami, and I had to say "no" and then I said, "Charles, I have a speaking date the day after we're being married!" And Charles said, "That's OK—where is it—we'll spend our honeymoon there." I hated to tell him it was at a Christian college in Lake Wales, Florida, where they would house us in the coed dorms, but praise the Lord, because of our mutual trust in God, he said that would be all right with him. However, for those who don't believe that God takes care of all the little details, this was the first speaking date in my entire career that had ever been canceled —and I learned just before our marriage that they had asked me for the wrong time because school was not in session on the 2nd of January.

There were so many people to meet, so many things to do, and so much getting acquainted that we had to do, that the time just flew by. Charles and I attended church on Christmas Eve where we shared communion together and Christmas Day we spent at the home of my son and his wife and baby. We spent part of the day visiting some friends, and the Lord used us together to bring a LIVING Christ into a heart. How we thanked God for giving us the greatest present he could think of—the opportunity of being used together in His Service. How our hearts thrilled! Charles said this was his greatest Christmas ever. It was interesting concerning Christmas gifts how God had tuned our minds into the same channel, because Charles gave me a watch and on the back of it is engraved an exact duplicate of the cover of "God Is Fabulous," and I gave him cuff links with the words "God Is Fabulous" engraved on them. It was a glorious time as we prayed together, read the Bible together, shared together, and drew closer and closer to God and to each other.

On Wednesday Charles went down to the courthouse to pick up the license, and I stayed home desperately trying to get my apartment cleaned out, and when he got to the county clerk's office and asked for the license, the clerk replied: "You can pick up your license on Friday morning, not today!" Charles almost panicked. He said, "That's too late—we're being married tonight." The conversation went something like this: "Well, I'm sorry, but because of the holiday it's not possible to get it before then." Then Charles asked to talk to the chief clerk who had told us on Monday that we could pick up the license, but was told he could pay for the license today and give them the blood tests, but the license wouldn't be available until Thursday morning at 9 A.M. at the very earliest. Charles explained that there were people coming from all over the United States and that we had to have the license, and finally the chief clerk said, "Well, here's a little slip—one of the judges in North Miami will give you your license tomorrow morning at 9 A.M. (New Year's Day)." Charles said, "That's too late . . . we're being married TONIGHT!"

Charles then asked if the judge was in, and if he

could have audience with him, but the chief clerk said he would talk to him for Charles, and Charles said the minute the chief clerk disappeared into the judge's chambers, he knew that three people were going to be in that room—the judge, the chief clerk and God, because he started praying, but he only got one word out . . . "GOD" . . . and as soon as he said it, he realized his total dependence upon God in this situation and he relaxed as he said, "I don't know what I'm worried about, God—I didn't set the wedding date—Frances certainly didn't set the wedding date—YOU did, so there's nothing for me to be concerned about," and with this a peace flooded Charles' soul.

After about fifteen minutes the clerk came out, took the slip away from Charles which entitled us to get our marriage license on Thursday morning, looked through a pile of slips, got another one out, scratched through the figure 9:A.M. January 1, 1970, and in its place wrote the following information: "12:01, January 1, 1970"—EXACTLY AS GOD HAD SAID.

I love reading the Old Testament where it quotes something that God said, and immediately after this is the statement "And it was so." That's all I could think of as Charles brought this little slip home. God spoke, AND IT WAS SO!

The P.T.L. (Party for the Lord) was beautiful—and spiritual (after all, I had promised Charles the most spiritual night of his life) and the wedding was most unusual. Under normal circumstances at my age I would have had a real private wedding, but since God had said it was to be at the Party for the

Lord, IT WAS SO! After the P.T.L., I slipped into the back of the church, changed into my wedding dress, and the entire wedding party sat on the front pew of the church. Charles and I had shared how we had met and how God had engineered the entire romance as our contribution to the P.T.L., and after the pastor gave a beautiful talk on love, he simply asked for the wedding party to step forward and we all stepped up to the front of the church.

Some people might have felt I was marrying a complete stranger because I had never had a date with Charles and really knew nothing about his personal life, but I stood there with no hesitation, no doubt, no qualms, no nothing except TRUST IN GOD and in his infinite wisdom and love. I knew as I stood there that God himself had ordained that I be Mrs. Charles Hunter and because it was wholly of God "IT WAS GOOD." Even though Charles and I are really just ordinary people (he's bald and I'm fat) many people said it was the most beautiful wedding they had ever seen because they saw "God in a wedding."

Many thoughts went through my mind on January 1, 1970. I remembered that God had said, "Seek ye FIRST the kingdom of God and his righteousness, and all these things shall be added unto you." And then I remembered "give, and it will be given to you; good measure, pressed down, shaken together, running over, will be put into your lap. For the measure you give will be the measure you get back." And because I had given all of my life to Him who can completely transform a life, he was giving me back far more than I ever could imagine. And I remem-

bered a paraphrase of Malachi where God said, "Try me, test me, prove me, and I will open the windows of heaven and shower down blessings far greater than you can contain." And how true this is. Even as I write this book, after the most glorious six months of my life, I never cease to be amazed at how God backs up his Word if we will only believe.

Many people were concerned as to what would happen to my speaking engagements after my marriage. God took care of this beautifully, too! God would not allow me to cancel a single engagement, nor would he let Charles stand in the way of my keeping every date that God had set up, so I left on my first tour only seven days after we were married. I was heartbroken at having to leave my beloved, and yet the call of God was stronger than anything in either of our lives, and since our love is filtered through Him, we bade each other good-bye through tears as I flew off to be where God called me; however, let me say that each tour has been a supreme blessing, has taught us many things, and most of all to be totally dependent upon God because His way is best. Somehow or other, God's grace surrounds both of us in a very special way each time I have to leave, and "His grace is sufficient for me." God knows how much we love each other, and God knows how much we hate being apart from each other, and in a magnificent way has allowed Charles to be with me on most of my trips where He has used us together in an exciting way.

We have just returned home after being at a youth camp together and speaking together in several churches, and as we returned to our home to celebrate our six months' anniversary, we thanked God for his love and his grace and his mercy which made all of this possible. We realize today that our marriage on January 1, 1970 was as complete a case of trusting God as anything in our life had ever been, because we really didn't even know what love actually was between the two of us. We merely believed God was doing it all, we trusted him for every detail, and we were running madly to keep up with the things he had scheduled for us, and really with no thought of whether or not we actually loved each other, but because we believe the promises of God's Word that he wants only the best for his children, we trusted him for the greatest decision of our lives, and as always, God never fails. Somehow in his great wisdom He brought two people together who had been through the fire and who came out of the fiery furnace saying, "We want to serve you and nothing else matters" . . . he brought two people together whose likes are so similar it's supernatural (but then God did it) . . . he brought two people together who love each other BECAUSE of Him . . . he brought two people together who needed each other, but didn't realize the need until God had done the job.

Charles still writes me daily when I'm away, although the letters are getting less and less because God provides for him to be with me, but on one of my tours, a letter had not arrived on schedule, and so I was without mail for the day. As I started to bed that night, I realized I had left one of Charles' letters in my suitcase from the trip before, so I decided to reread it in place of a new letter. As I read I discovered the most magnificent love letter I have ever *read—and while it's written in Charles' beautiful handwriting, I'm sure that God himself wrote the letter, and so I'm sharing it with you with a prayer that because of a romance and marriage that God engineered in 1970, you will look at your own marriage, your own home and your own life.*

We put Christ FIRST in our lives, FIRST in our marriage, and FIRST in our home, and we believe this is the reason that God has blessed us so mightily.

*   *   *

My dearest, dear Sweetheart,

Love knows no bounds and it is the most powerful word in the Bible except *God* and *Christ Jesus*. Actually *Love* is the thread that weaves together God the Father, God the Son and God the Holy Spirit, and then that same thread of Love ties our spirits, wholly belonging to God, into the same oneness as the triune Godhead. "As I am in you, Father and you in me" so are you and I, Sweetheart, one in Christ and one made of two who were brought into one spirit, one body and one soul directly and entirely by God, and so acting as "one" we will serve God and proclaim Christ Jesus every day for the rest of our lives together.

I love you with a love astoundingly more profound than I ever believed was possible, fully recognizing that this is only so because it is that "God Love" which really exists in us and in the same perfect image of God in which we were created, God gives us the same PERFECT love he gave to Adam and Eve, but which was taken away to be made less than perfect because of sin in their lives. How beautifully rich are the fresh treasures God gave us when he reached into his great storehouse, opened the windows of heaven and poured them into our bodies, minds and souls! Why shouldn't we love God through Christ completely, and yet *we had to have a complete desire to want Him more than anything else in life before He could assume total control of our lives.* Yes, we love our God more than anything else or all things combined in this world. May God hear these words as a prayer tonite as 12:01 just passed, twenty-four days since he made us one! I love Him and I love you, Sweetheart—all as one single love. I'm jubilantly happy even with you 1,200 miles away, but nearer to me than my own hands.

Your
Charles

*　　*　　*

AUTHOR'S NOTE: To God be the Glory, great things He has done!